Win More Business

Write Better Proposals

By: Michel Theriault

WoodStone Press
Toronto, Canada

This book is dedicated to my wife, Melanie.

First Edition

ISBN 978-0-9813374-0-1

Published 2010 by WoodStone Press

Preface

When writing proposals, the goal is to persuade prospective clients that you're better than the competition. But winning business is about more than just offering an empty sales pitch. You must develop clear, concise and compelling proposals that illustrate the benefits of your service offering and demonstrate your capabilities.

It sounds simple, but your competition is trying to do the same thing. This book gives you the edge you need to beat them.

The strategies and techniques in this book come from many years of experience writing both successful and unsuccessful proposals. While many of the proposals I wrote were successful and increased the company's size and revenues, every proposal was a learning experience.

The techniques also come from my experience writing Request for Proposal documentation for corporate and government clients as well as evaluating RFP submissions for them. My experience on the client side provided firsthand evidence about what works and what doesn't.

Along the way, I've refined the approaches and concepts through my research on business communications, selling and persuasion. The research also allowed me to understand why the techniques work.

Whether you write short proposals or long, complex responses to formal RFPs, this book will help you write them better. Even if you've been writing proposals for years, you'll discover new ways to develop and write proposals that will win more business.

Clients and buyers will also benefit from this book. By understanding how successful companies develop their proposals, your evaluation task will be easier and you may even change the way you write your RFP to make it easier and get better results.

Michel Theriault

Table of Contents

Winning is Everything **1**

Using this Book to Win More Proposals 2

Part 1 Write a Winning Proposal **3**

Be Strategic 4
What Skills Do You Need? 5
What Makes a Winning Proposal? 7
What Makes a Losing Proposal? 17
Do You Know Why You Lost? 22
Alphabet Soup – RFPs and More 24
The Eight Golden Rules for a Successful Proposal 28
Summary 29

Part 2 Survival of the Fittest **31**

The Process 32
Manage the Process, Don't Let it Manage You 46
Surviving the Site Tour and Bidders Meetings 46
Herding Cats 48
Pulling Teeth 49
Reality Check – The Red Team 51
Your Proposal Team 54
Summary 57

Part 3 Prepare for Battle – Strategy for Success **59**

It's More Than Just Writing a Proposal 60
Develop Your Response Strategy 60
If You Aren't Sure, Ask 72
Dissecting the RFP 73

What You Need to Do to Get to the Table 79
Playing the Game – Evaluation Scoring 83
Get Your Couch – You Need an Analysis 85
Help the Client Help Themselves 88
How Do You Respond to a Bad RFP? 89
Go Bold or Go Home 94
Cafeteria Pricing 95
Surviving Bad Situations 98
Summary 105

Part 4 Figuring Out What the Client Really Wants 107

Do You Know What the Client Wants? 108
Do They Really Care About Value-Added? 113
Can You Give Them What They Need? 115
Espionage, the Modern (and Legal) Way 118
Care and Feeding of Evaluators 120
Don't Let Perception Overwhelm Reality 122
Why Would They Want to Work With You? 124
Summary 127

Part 5 If You Can't Sell, Go Home 129

Can You Sell What You're Selling? 130
Sell the Steak as Well as the Sizzle 133
It's Not About You – It's About Them 134
Ghosts Can Lead to Success 135
Making Your Message Stick 137
Mirroring 140
Assess and Target the Evaluators 141
Ask Yourself Critical Questions for Success 142
Answer the Question the Client Doesn't Ask 144
Do You Adapt to the Proposal Style? 145
Summary 155

Part 6 It's All About the Content 157

One-Size-Fits-All is Not a Winning Strategy 158
Bigger is Not Better 160
For the Prosecution – It's All About the Evidence 160
So, What Have You Done For Me Lately? 162
Answer the Damn Question! 164
A Picture is Worth More Than 1,000 Words 166
Don't Put Too Much Junk in the Trunk 167
Get Rid of the Clutter 170
They Didn't Ask? Tell Them Anyway! 171
Telling Stories 172
Extracting Material from SMEs and Subcontractors 173
Compliance Matrix 174
Summary 178

Part 7 Getting it All On Paper 179

The Elements of Successful Proposal Writing 180
What You're Up Against 180
Avoid Disaster – Start with an Outline 183
Build in the Message 184
How Much Should You Write? 184
Write to Communicate 186
Do You Have Any Idea How to Write and Edit? 192
Writing to Persuade, Not Sedate 193
Write From the Client's Point of View 195
Too Much Detailed Information 196
Are You Still Using a Typewriter? 197
Should You Use a Professional Writer? 199
Use a Writing Process 200
Win With Format and Structure 202
Your Writing Style Matters 208
Go Fishing 212

Managing the Production Process 213
Summary 215

Part 8 Things Clients Want You to Know 217

Differentiate Yourself 218
Skip the Sales Pitch 218
Follow the Format 219
Understand the Requirements 220
Don't Assume Familiarity 221
Don't Give Us Marketing Fluff 221
Show Us That You Care 222
Don’t Use Boilerplate Material 223
What Not to Do 224
Summary 226

Quick Reference Material 227

References 241

Index 243

Winning is Everything

The only reason you write proposals is to win more business.

Winning means getting a client to choose your proposal over your competitor's. While the financial proposal carries a lot of weight, a compelling written proposal will tilt the odds in your favor. You may even win more business without having the lowest price.

A clear strategy for winning is the foundation for writing a successful proposal. The proposal is your primary communication tool with a prospective client, and you don't usually get a chance to explain, elaborate or clarify what you write.

Developing a strategy will provide a clear, concise and compelling message that's easy to evaluate. You'll take into account the client's needs, position your company's benefits in their eyes, use your competition's weaknesses and strengths to your advantage, and provide information that demonstrates and justifies why you're the best choice.

Your proposal must convey all this to your prospective client so that the proposal is easy to evaluate, and you're awarded the highest possible evaluation score.

This book will provide you with insight and strategies you can use to improve your proposals and win more business with less effort.

Using this Book to Win More Proposals

This book is split into a number of parts that cover key areas of proposal writing.

The first part provides an overview of some of the topics covered in more depth later in the book. Since some key themes cross various strategies, they appear in several parts with details that focus on the specific strategy.

The parts following the overview provide techniques for developing and writing a successful proposal. These involve key areas including managing your proposal response, understanding the client, developing your strategy, structuring your proposal for maximum impact and how to actually write your proposal so it's persuasive and compelling.

The last part of the book includes things clients want you to know before you write and submit your proposal. These come directly from clients and support the techniques provided in the book, as well as providing additional advice.

After each part, there's a short summary along with a place for you to list what you need to do differently to win more business with your proposals. I encourage you to write on the summary page, make notes throughout the book, and highlight information for easy reference. That's what this book is for.

I've also reproduced the lists and checklists from the book and included them separately so you can photocopy or even cut out the pages to use in your next proposal. Some of the material is also available on our website. For more information on where to get the online material, see the last page of the book.

What Skills Do You Need?

Subject Matter Expert

To write an effective proposal response, you need qualified subject matter experts (SME) who contribute to or write key elements of the technical portion of the proposal. Using writers from the business development or sales team or even hiring external writers is tempting, however you'll end up with generalities and something that looks and feels more like a sales pitch rather than solid quantifiable details and information that evaluators need in order to give you a good score.

There's no substitute for someone who understands the business and knows how it works in practice. The other benefit of having that expertise is that SMEs can draw on their past. They can bring forward issues that may be important to the client, but which a non-technical writer simply won't be able to include.

Subject matter experts include individuals within your organization who are highly experienced in a particular area, such as quality assurance, human resources, Information Technology (IT), logistics, product development or direct service delivery. Subject matter experts can also be subcontractors who provide a particular part of the overall service.

Even the best subject matter experts, however, may not write well or be able to focus their knowledge and expertise into strategic messages directed at proposal evaluators. In this case, use the SME's knowledge and expertise, and support them with someone who can do the writing.

Marketing and sales skills

While the technical subject matter expert is important, the ability to sell is equally important. Be careful however – your proposal can't simply be a marketing and sales pitch.

You need to be able to combine your technical and service expertise with client requirements, deliver on hot buttons, themes and messages, and talk about the technical subject matter in a way that gets the client's attention and speaks directly to the evaluator in a concise, well-structured response that results in a high evaluation score.

The necessary skills go beyond general marketing and sales and delve into specifics related to your particular service and how to best represent your capabilities so they match client expectations, evaluation criteria and the RFP questions and structure.

Effective selling involves being able to look at your service, solution, background and expertise, and identify ways to take the facts and turn them into compelling reasons for the client to favor your proposal over the competition's.

Creative skills

Writing a proposal is not a mechanical process. It requires creativity in addressing issues, dealing with negative concerns, putting forward your advantages, and convincing the client you have the best proposal.

Creativity doesn't mean using a template document, boilerplate material and cut-and-paste response. Creativity enables you to uniquely address the requirements of the proposal by using base material, but not simply by reusing old material. Every proposal should be customized for the client, but that doesn't mean just doing a 'search and replace' on the client's name.

To some extent, creativity also involves the ability to look at what you've got, compare it to what's expected, and match up those results in a creative way, especially when there's a gap.

Tip When there's an area in which you don't have direct experience or background, being creative will help you find ways to address the problem effectively, and meet requirements as closely as possible.

How you present information, including diagrams, lists, tables and photos, also benefits from creativity. Since the only reason for including information of any kind is to influence the evaluator to give you the highest evaluation score possible, you need to be creative in your presentation. Resist the temptation to use information in its original form, and understand why you're presenting it. Then modify your presentation to get the point across.

Writing

Good writing skills go well beyond grammar and punctuation. In fact, good writers can write bad proposals.

The writing skills you need include the ability to get the message across in a concise targeted fashion with simple, well-crafted writing that's not pretentious or arrogant. This sometimes means ignoring rules you learned in English 101. Communicating effectively is more important, because the message needs to be easily read and understood by the evaluator.

Filling pages with colorful prose, complex vocabulary, and complicated but correct grammatical structure that impresses rather than communicates won't help you win proposals. At the same time, filling your proposal with poorly written, highly-technical and unfocussed writing is also sure to fail.

The gap between what you write and how the client interprets your writing is a hurdle you need to overcome.

What Makes a Winning Proposal?

The major challenge is determining how to present a convincing and honest proposal without falling into the trap of making it look like just another sales pitch.

The following strategies all contribute to a successful proposal and should be considered when writing.

Addresses the client's needs

The reason you write the proposal is to address a client's needs. That's why it's important for you to fully understand what the client really needs.

Unfortunately, clients themselves may not know and may not have outlined their needs very well in the RFP documents. Even if it seems like the client provided enough information, try to understand the client and their needs beyond what's written in the RFP document.

Doing some research about the company is the only way to understand its needs. Techniques are discussed in Part 4.

Knowing what the client's needs are, however, does not guarantee you'll address those needs effectively in your proposal. To be compelling, you need a strategy, and you need to clearly describe the right solution.

Convincing, yet balanced

A winning proposal must be convincing yet balanced. While the purpose is to sell yourself, fluff and unbelievable claims on the sales job can easily turn off a potential client, and will certainly make the client reconsider the validity of your claims.

You must provide evidence of the strength of your abilities and background, and sell those based on the client's needs. The proposal must be based on realistic and convincing arguments that demonstrate rather than simply make claims.

Example

This isn't convincing. It sounds like hollow marketing fluff:

"Our methodology is an approach for business alignment that helps our team and our clients realize the highest return. We do this by ensuring employees understand and accept the roles and tasks to which they're assigned, incorporate our client's values for professional standards, and adhere to our strict values."

The most convincing argument includes admitting or identifying problems and clearly showing how they can be overcome and mitigated. An honest and helpful approach adds credibility.

A common part of a winning proposal is demonstrating that you can do the job, that you understand the client's needs, and that you have the necessary experience, resources and skills to perform the service. Your ability to convince the client means the difference between a winning and a losing proposal.

Credibility

Credibility will influence how the client scores your proposal. Credibility means what you say is believable and has been demonstrated by your past history and the results you achieved for other clients.

There's often a temptation to fill proposals with general statements, hyperbole and marketing fluff. But without facts and evidence, these will be seen for exactly what they are – a sales pitch. Establishing credibility early in your proposal will lend additional weight to everything you say. All it takes is one false or unbelievable claim to destroy your credibility.

Example

This is a claim that isn't supported by credible evidence:

"John is a recognized leader in the industry, combining in-depth knowledge of the technical processes with an extensive business management background. He has been an integral part of our management team for more than 14 years."

The simple question the client will ask is - *recognized by whom*?

Credibility is built through demonstrating experience and results that can be quantified and proven. As soon as you put doubt into the client's minds about what you're saying, they stop believing you.

It's also about wording. If you use weasel words and loose language to either qualify a statement or suggest ambiguity about your accomplishments, experience, approach or commitment to what you're proposing, your statement loses credibility.

Credibility is about more than just what you put in your proposal. Your organization must have a reputation that supports what you're saying.

There are very few organizations with stellar, unblemished reputations. The question is simply – in what areas is there doubt? Some of those areas can be pervasive and damaging, and could undermine what you're trying to say. In which case, the client may not score you very well in certain areas because of it.

Simple Rules

You can also lose credibility with bold, unproven claims. Avoid these claims unless you can support them:

- ✖ "Leader in the Industry..."
- ✖ "Award Winning..."
- ✖ "Best in Class..."
- ✖ "Industry Recognized..."
- ✖ "Proven Processes..."
- ✖ "State of the Art....
- ✖ "World Class...."
- ✖ "Highly Qualified..."

Credibility includes the perception outsiders have of your company, whether true or not. It's important to fully understand the industry and the community's perception of your organization, and instead of dismissing them, deal with the issues head-on.

Example

Your reputation has an impact

If you have a reputation of treating people poorly, then a client who needs you to transition their employees into your organization may have reservations.

Questions about service or product quality, and assumptions about your performance in the market, will override any statements you make about your abilities. They will override any quality management or quality assurance procedures you say you have in place, and they will override any claims you make about quality – the client simply won't believe you. If you address this problem directly, for example, by admitting you had problems in the past and you've made quantifiable changes, you can mitigate these negative perceptions.

Tip

Social media, blogs and other sources of information have the potential to damage your reputation overnight. When necessary, vigorously defend your reputation online, and always assume someone in your prospective client's office has searched for information about your company. If a search reveals negative stories and opinions, take efforts to counter these in your proposal.

It's very important to look critically at your organization. If there are any problems with your credibility or reputation, address them up front and frankly. By leaving doubt about your company's credibility in the mind of the clients, you're creating doubt about your entire proposal.

Capture the client's attention

The writing itself has to grab a client's attention and maintain it while you lead them to the important points in your proposal. You must make it easy for the client to both see what you have to say, and evaluate you without having to dig for information.

Getting the client's attention requires compelling information, facts, examples and stories. Telling stories about examples, other clients, implementation, problem solving and successes you have had is more powerful than general discussion and marketing material.

Include real world examples and stories from your experience that illustrate how you did something beyond scope, how your knowledge or resources helped a client at a time of crisis, or how your innovations improved a client's competitive position in their own marketplace. If necessary, change the names in the story to protect confidentiality, but offer to provide details or contact information if you can.

Example

These are examples of stories you can use to capture the client's attention and provide evidence to support what you've said in your proposal:

- ✓ Your response to emergency situations on behalf of the client saved them money.
- ✓ How you met an incredibly short timeline for delivering a product to a client, who needed it to fulfill their own customer's order.
- ✓ How you introduced new technology or processes that benefited the client with reduced costs, improved process, or shorter delivery times.
- ✓ How you discovered an error or issue outside of your scope and advised the client, thereby saving the client costs or embarrassment.

The ability to capture the client's attention in key areas that create a positive impression of your proposal is what makes the difference between winning and losing.

The other way to get the client's attention is by writing about your benefits in a way that matters to the client. A common mistake is to identify the features of your proposal and talk about what you do and how well you do it without clearly explaining the benefits the client receives. Don't assume the client will read about your features or even benefits and immediately connect those with their own needs. You have to explain it to the client and tell them why it matters.

Lesson Learned

This was a wasted opportunity:

An RFP response provided a list of reports available to the client, but failed to mention why the reports would be useful or what benefits the reports provided over the competition.

Be sure to actually quantify your benefits. Extend the benefit into the client's organization by helping the client understand how it impacts them and telling them with facts and numbers. This approach makes it easier for the client to imagine how they will actually benefit from what you can do for them. This technique will get more attention than general statements and claims.

Example

This statement provides detailed, results-oriented information for the client:

"Our proposed solution reduces your labor by 30 minutes for each unit you produce. At 100,000 units a year, that's a 50,000-hour labor reduction, or up to $1,000,000 in cost savings per year based on typical industry labor rates."

Make their reading easy

Reviewing proposals is tedious and sometimes boring. Make it easier for the client to read your proposal and absorb key information that will help the evaluators score your proposal.

The reality is that we're all challenged to thoroughly understand and remember what we read. This has nothing to do with how smart we are, it has more to do with the effort it takes to read through material and pick out the things that are important.

Imagine the task in front of the client's evaluators. They need to review and absorb vast quantities of material from a variety of bidders and decide which ones best meet their needs.

Sometimes evaluators will have a formal scoring framework to work with, and sometimes they won't. But even with the best scoring framework, we rely on humans to interpret and perceive the information we present to them, and to make judgments by allocating a score based on specific criteria and a scoring framework.

To get the best results from your written proposal, keep this in mind. Make it easy for the client to see the information that matters by putting it front and centre, and easy to find.

This isn't simply about words. It's about visually organizing your proposal so your message is seen and understood. Organize your material in a format they can be easily absorbed and that relates to the scoring criteria.

Clarity

The information in your proposal needs to be completely clear to the client. Clarity includes eliminating or reducing unnecessary information, and providing a quick summary of the key points in any section before getting into details, particularly if the details are complex or technical.

Sometimes you need to include long, complex examples or information, however including those in the main body detracts from the main points and makes the proposal much harder to read.

The best approach, if it's allowed, is to include the material in an appendix. However, simply including the material in an appendix and referring to it in the main body of your proposal is a lost opportunity. Instead, provide an introduction to explain the information and why it demonstrates you have the experience and depth of knowledge.

Be careful about cross-referencing information. The cross reference shouldn't include the core information and message, which should be exactly where the evaluators need to see it. Cross-referenced information should only be supporting information that evaluators can access if they want to.

Every time you send the evaluator to another part of the document to find important material, you're interrupting the flow of thought and possibly losing their attention, something that's required to get a good evaluation.

Lessons Learned

Don't send the evaluator to the appendix for key information:

When an RFP requested a detailed project timeline the proposal writer included it in an appendix on large, foldout pages.

The writer simply directed the evaluators to the appendix without providing a summary in the main proposal and without touching on the key parts of the timeline, milestones and completion dates that the client obviously cared about. By understanding the key client issues around the schedule, the important information could have been provided in the proposal while also meeting RFP requirements.

Highlight the key or significant issues and even include a short version, no longer than a page in length, to provide an overview. Describe the benefits the detailed information demonstrates and how it relates to client requirements. Focus attention on scoring criteria if relevant.

Remember, the individuals reviewing the proposal may not have the same interest in details. Some may only want high-level information and won't look at the details, whether in an appendix or not. Others will closely review the appendix and appreciate your level of detail and thoroughness.

In either case, by providing the context and a summary, you'll be able to convey the reasons the information is important, and why it gives you an advantage. This is one way your proposal can address the issue of multiple reviewers and ensure your message is clear to all of them.

Having a competitive advantage

You can write the best proposal, but if you don't have some sort of competitive advantage you can talk about, you're less likely to win, all things being equal. Your competitive advantage factors into two parts of your proposal.

The first part is pricing. Your advantage could be volume that reduces unit costs, or a unique technology that cuts costs. Your advantage could also be better knowledge, experience or systems, which lets you use fewer resources, be more efficient, and generally reduce costs throughout your processes and approach to the product or service.

The second part is your service or product capabilities. While your services or product may be the reason you have a price advantage, there are probably other reasons you're a benefit to the client and why you have an advantage over your competitor. You need to identify and highlight these advantages – don't assume the client will recognize them.

But just having the advantage isn't enough. You need to demonstrate why those advantages are important to the client, what benefits they'll receive, and make it easy for the client to understand why they should have what you're offering. You need to assess where they fit within the RFP or proposal process, and ensure they're clearly identified in the right sections where they'll be evaluated and scored accordingly.

All of your competitive advantages need to be analyzed for how and why they would matter to the client. Unless it has a price advantage or it's something that really matters to the client, the competitive advantage simply isn't important and shouldn't be emphasized.

If your competitive advantage simply provides a "value add" to the client, assess whether this advantage will improve your score and win the bid. Based on that evaluation, devote the appropriate amount of time in your proposal to discussing and selling competitive advantages that matter. Be sure your competitive advantage is truly unique and not the same as your competition's.

Example

Make sure your advantage is truly an advantage:

To demonstrate innovation, a bidder highlighted their new technique and promoted it as an innovative concept. In reality, the entire industry was switching to this new technique. Not only was this no longer an advantage, the company's credibility suffered because of the false claim.

Without a competitive advantage that matters to the client, spending time discussing it in your proposal won't help you win, and will water down other more important messages. Focus your attention and devote space in your proposal to things that matter to the client.

What Makes a Losing Proposal?

We tend to focus so much on what wins proposals that we seldom try to understand why we lose them. Lessons from losses will always have more impact on future success than lessons from winning, so always spend some time thinking about what didn't work, and do it differently in the next proposal.

Show little understanding of the client's problem

When you ignore what the client has told you either verbally or in the formal RFP documents, and you simply put forward a proposal and a solution that doesn't specifically and concretely address their needs and concerns, then you'll be relegated to the bottom of the pile and somebody else will win the proposal.

The only reason the client is asking for a proposal is to solve a problem or address a need. You may think you understand the client's problem and are solving their needs, but it's more important than that. You have to make it clear within your proposal that you understand the client's needs and how you're solving their problem.

One way to do this is to mirror back the client's problems and what they've said in the RFP, thereby acknowledging you've understood their problem and are addressing it. Don't overdo this, since the client won't appreciate whole paragraphs that look like they were lifted from the RFP documents. Keep it short, paraphrase the client, and position to acknowledge the client's issues and present your solutions.

Superficial research

It's obvious when a proposal response uses superficial or generic information as part of its solution and technical response.

You need to demonstrate a unique solution that's better than your competitor's, and is designed specifically for the client. This means including details that show you understand the client's needs, and have done your research and gathered background information.

What may appear to be unimportant information can help support your proposal. When the client reads it, your proposal will seem much more personal.

This could include incorporating the proper name of the system the client currently uses, and using specific titles, names and other information to show you understand the client. Use key phrases and terminology that the client uses within annual reports, news releases and other documentation.

Example

The value of good research:

For a proposal that included a 1-800 number to receive requests for a specific service, research showed that the client already had their own internal process for receiving requests. This information was included in the proposal text and in a flowchart, demonstrating the proposal writers understood how the client was organized and could design a process to fit within their existing workflow.

Insufficient expertise or experience

Not demonstrating the expertise and experience the client expects from you is a sure way to lose a proposal.

Simply put, the client is looking for a solution to a problem. If you don't have the experience necessary to provide those solutions with little or no risk to the client, they'll likely consider somebody else.

The question is whether you actually lack experience and expertise, or are simply not able to demonstrate it. If you dig deeply within your organization and your company's past experience, you may find expertise within your existing resources, including staff and subcontractors, or within current projects or products that parallel the experience needed for this particular proposal.

Example

Dealing with a lack of experience:

While a company had sufficient experience and expertise in the required service, they hadn't served the specific business segment yet.

A review of internal resumes found an existing employee who had experience in that business segment, and that person was added to the transition team. In addition, experience in other business segments was examined to see what characteristics were shared with the new business segment. Experience with these common characteristics was emphasized in the proposal response using a table that compared their experiences with the needs of the client.

By finding those nuggets of experience and expertise, and clearly describing how they support your current solution with little or no risk to the client, you'll be in a better position to win the RFP.

You can also partner with another company that has the skills and experience you lack. This way, you can emphasize the benefits of both companies. You may need to clearly identify the partnership or subcontractor relationship in your proposal, but when writing the response, make sure you come across as a single, cohesive service provider. If there are different sections or questions related to the various organization's expertise, they must be written so they have the same approach, look and feel. If they're disjointed, you'll lose points with the evaluators.

Failure to respond to client needs

Not responding to client requirements as they're stated in the RFP, or as they appear based on your own research of the underlying requirements, is a sure recipe for failure.

The client has asked for proposals specifically to address their needs. If you don't describe how your solution, expertise and experience will address the client's needs, you have not met the basic requirement for the proposal.

Lesson Learned

It's about the client, not you:

A losing proposal failed to respond to the client's needs because it was too inward-looking, focusing more on the attributes of the supplier's company. It didn't relate the supplier's abilities to the client's needs. Instead, it included a typical boilerplate solution and material that was not customized to the client's specific situation. It was simply too generic.

If you don't specifically address and discuss client needs, and how your solution dovetails into their requirements by mirroring back the client's own language, expectations, terminology and problems you're solving, somebody else will.

Hard to understand, evaluate

Many people write to impress rather than to communicate. They use long, complex sentences, and words that most of us have to look up in the dictionary. While this may work well in a thesis or scientific paper, it doesn't work in the business world, and it doesn't work in proposals.

The only reason to write a proposal is to communicate your ideas and your solutions so the client can tie them back to their own requirements and choose you over somebody else.

Unless you make your ideas and solutions easy to see, evaluators will miss them. Evaluators have to review large amounts of text, remember what they read, and link that with a scoring system that helps them choose a supplier. If you make evaluators search for information, or skim over important information because the text is difficult to read, they won't be able to find the information they need to score you properly.

Inconsistent response

Your proposal response will reflect your organization. If you're inconsistent in your answers or in how you represent your company, products, services or solutions, the client is likely to notice.

In particular, if your proposal has different sections written by various internal staff or subcontractors, and these sections are inconsistent in terminology, approach, look and feel, then the client will see that you're not providing a single cohesive service, and question your ability to integrate and manage various resources.

In addition, if you provide information that conflicts with information in the proposal itself, or with other published information, such as your website or annual report, you risk having the client recognize the inconsistency and questioning your credibility.

The proposal is an opportunity for you to demonstrate how easy it will be to work with you. Even if you have different subcontractors, suppliers and service providers as part of your team, or if various individuals write your proposal, you need to consolidate and edit the material to maintain a consistent, unified look and feel.

Do You Know Why You Lost?

Everyone loses proposals, but do you know why you're losing them?

Most clients are willing to provide feedback as part of the process. This involves debriefing the bidders, either in a formal meeting or informally on the phone.

If the formal approach is an option, make sure you take advantage of it, and make sure the right people from your company are at the table when the debriefing occurs. You also need to share the feedback with those involved in the bid process so they can understand what worked and what didn't to improve the next proposal.

When being debriefed on a losing proposal, try to understand how the client interpreted and perceived what you presented compared to the way in which you intended it to be perceived. It's not always what you say and how you say it, it's also how the client interprets it.

Lessons Learned

Don't assume they know you:

I've read proposal responses from companies that I know quite well, yet the proposal response does not reflect the capabilities or background and experience of the company. As a result, the companies are putting themselves at a huge disadvantage simply because they don't understand how they come across in a proposal.

If the RFP process doesn't include a debriefing, contact the client and ask for one. The client should be willing to discuss their reaction to your technical bid, even if they won't reveal your score or where you placed relative to the competition.

Rather than simply sitting and listening, ask probing questions. Ask about things that you could have done, and whether they would have been received differently. Ask the clients what you need to do differently to get their attention in the future.

The clients are unlikely to share or discuss pricing, however they may give you an indication of how much pricing played a part in the selection, depending on how the RFP itself was structured and scored.

Don't be afraid to ask hard questions, and don't resist listening to honest responses. That's one of the most important ways to learn and improve for next time.

Of course, you need to consider that not all clients are the same. The way one client evaluates or perceives your proposal may be different from another. Take everything in context. By getting more debriefs, you'll begin to understand what key elements of your proposal process you must change to be more successful.

Tip Feedback may be embarrassing or hard to accept, but make sure you share it with the key people involved in proposal responses. Implementing feedback will improve future proposals.

When you seek feedback, you should also try to get feedback on things that were outside of your written proposal, such as the client's general impression of your company, and their opinion of the oral presentations that were part of the process.

In addition to getting debriefs on losing proposals, ask new clients why you won, and get feedback from them about your proposal. This will complement and/or confirm the feedback you receive on the losing proposals. Ask your new client what they liked and didn't like about your proposal.

Alphabet Soup – RFPs and More

There are more than just RFPs. You need to apply the same approaches and some of the processes in the steps that lead up to an RFP as you do for the RFP itself. By understanding, in particular, the RFI, REOI and RFQ, and how they help you get invited to bid on an RFP, you'll be better prepared both to be invited and to influence the final RFP document.

Request for Information (RFI)

The RFI is typically used when a client wants to gather information from the market to help develop an RFP approach, make decisions about the procurement process, and help develop the RFP document and even the scope.

The RFI presents an opportunity to try to shape the client's final RFP to your benefit. Take the opportunity to identify approaches, bundling of scope, pricing structure, technology the client should request, and any other elements you would like to see in the final RFP that will give you an edge over your competition. Take the process seriously, and use the same techniques you would in a proposal to convince the client that the information and suggestions you're providing should be incorporated in the final RFP.

Request for Expressions of Interest (REOI)

This process is used to identify potential bidders and establish their level of interest. It is issued in advance of an RFP and should include enough information for you to decide whether you're likely to pursue the final RFP. If this will be followed by an RFQ process, keep it light and focused on client requirements. However, if the client will be going straight to an RFP, you need to demonstrate that you should be included in the RFP process, otherwise there's a risk you may not be on the client's final list for the RFP.

Request for Qualification (RFQ)

This step is used by the client to pre-qualify bidders and narrow the field to a small number of companies who will receive the RFP itself. It's usually a shorter, simpler process that's open to all interested service providers. It uses a straightforward series of questions and qualification requirements that require lower effort to evaluate than a full RFP, and does not include pricing or require identification of a final solution.

Organizations required to conduct a public bidding process use the RFQ to narrow down the list of bidders invited to respond to the RFP, and minimize the number of RFPs they'll need to evaluate. Even with organizations not required to use public procurement processes, RFQs are used when the number of capable bidders is too large to manage in an RFP process.

An RFQ process minimizes the level of effort you need to make as a bidder, and prevents you from expending efforts on an RFP you aren't likely to win. But while it's a shorter, simpler process, you need to employ a process similar to the one you use for an RFP since it's just as important. If you don't pass the RFQ process, you will be eliminated from further consideration.

It's important to note that some organizations use the acronym RFQ for a different purpose, known as a Request for Quote. This is similar to a tender where your response is evaluated based on price and some mandatory requirements such as bonding and insurance. A formal written submission is seldom required.

Request for Proposal (RFP)

The RFP is a flexible process usually used for services where the delivery of services can be accomplished with various approaches. The RFP structure and approach can vary widely, so reading the documentation is important to understand the process being used by the client, including procurement rules, evaluation processes, and negotiations.

Rather than predefining the methods of delivering the service, the Client provides required guidelines and outcomes and allows the bidder to design a solution that meets their needs. The requirements will vary widely. Some have a very detailed scope of work or even detailed specifications for certain areas, while others are very general and broad, requiring a great deal of interpretation and a wider range of possible solutions.

The approach will depend on the client's specific situation and how much they want – or are able to – define their requirements. The requirements are often outcome-based and may include some form of service level agreements and performance measurements, with a financial risk/reward structure.

The RFP process may include negotiation of the technical solution and pricing. A proposal that suits the client's needs but has some details the client may prefer to do differently can be negotiated with changes. A preferred bidder may have a higher price that exceeds the client's budget and may be negotiated, either with smaller margins or by changing the elements of the solution or scope to bring the price down.

Sole Source

This method is typically used for lower value procurement initiatives that require unique or specialized services. These may be available from only one company, or where a specific supplier's knowledge, experience or approach has a great deal of value to the service being required. Even organizations required to use an open, competitive process are sometimes able to procure using this method if it meets their procurement policies and fits within certain criteria.

This method is quick and easy for the client, but requires the bidder to fully understand the requirements and still provide a compelling proposal, not only to convince the client they have chosen the right company, but also to provide the evidence they need to justify their decision.

Request for Quotation (RFQ)

The RFQ is sometimes used for low to medium-valued procurement requirements where the requirements are clearly defined and well understood, and where a competitive pricing process is required. Often a select number of known companies are asked to quote, but sometimes the client will add in some new ones. The only requirement from the bidders is a price, which typically provides the basis for the decision. The RFQ itself is usually a very short description of the work and other related requirements, sufficient for the bidders to provide a quotation. The quote may be for a fixed price or for time and materials.

Request for Tender (RFT)

A Tender is typically used for defined requirements, which enable the bidder to provide a firm price based on clear, detailed specifications. While some written response may be required in addition to the pricing, it's more for compliance and to validate qualifications than to evaluate a proposed solution. The lowest price is typically the winning bid as long as compliance and qualifications meet requirements. There are either built-in criteria for compliance and qualifications, or only known bidders are invited to participate in the tender. An RFQ process may precede the RFT to provide for the compliance and qualification stage, with the RFT evaluated solely on price.

This approach is commonly used for construction projects and commodity products rather than for services, however some services may also lend themselves to this type of procurement approach.

Government procurement

If you respond to government RFP's at any level, there are often much stricter and more formal processes involved in the procurement initiatives. You should familiarize yourself with the legislation and policy that governs the government's procurement initiatives so you understand the restrictions and follow the rules, including cross-border trade agreements.

The Eight Golden Rules for a Successful Proposal

Here are eight simple rules you should use when writing proposals – they will help you focus your efforts and give the client what they expect:

1. Follow instructions when responding to the RFP.
2. Understand what the client wants to hear.
3. Answer the questions the client asks.
4. Have a great solution that solves the client's problem.
5. Be creative about your proposal and solution.
6. Keep the sales pitch to a dull roar.
7. Get your message across clearly and concisely.
8. Make it easy for evaluators to evaluate you positively.

Summary

Writing a proposal isn't just about writing. A lot of additional effort is required before you can get to the point of putting pen to paper. And in most RFPs, being strategic in how you respond will increase your chances of success.

Techniques You Can Use:

- ✓ Make sure you understand the client and their needs.
- ✓ Provide a convincing, compelling reason for them to choose you.
- ✓ Make your proposal clear and easy to evaluate.
- ✓ Answer the questions.

Traps To Avoid:

- ✖ Don't make it hard for the client to see your advantages.
- ✖ Don't be inconsistent in your proposal responses.
- ✖ Don't assume this client is the same as the others.

Your Action Plan to Write Better Proposals:

Based on this chapter, list several things you need to do to win more business with your proposals.

Priority	Things to Do

Part 2
Survival of the Fittest

A successful proposal response can take considerable effort, requiring your sustained attention as well as attracting the interest, cooperation and help of other people in your organization who are also focused on day-to-day responsibilities.

Even if you have a business development team to support you on larger proposals, you still need a plan to be successful.

The following are among the techniques outlined in this section:

- Treat your proposal like a project and develop a plan.
- Develop the overall structure before starting on the pieces.
- Take control of the process and resources you need.
- Understand clearly what you need to be successful.

> *"What does not destroy me, makes me stronger."*
>
> *– Friedrich Nietzsche, 1889*

The Process

A successful proposal follows a process. The details depend on the proposal type, size and complexity, yet a structure is still necessary. This may involve a check-off sheet you use for a short proposal to keep organized and track key elements, or a complex process involving various departments, subcontractors and a proposal team.

The key steps in a successful proposal response process include these elements, which will be expanded further below:

1. Pre-RFP issue
2. RFP review
3. Strategy
4. Kick-off
5. Pricing Model
6. Service solution
7. Management solution
8. Style sheet
9. Project plan (resources and schedule)
10. Version control
11. Iteration and consolidation
12. Production and delivery

1. Pre-RFP issue

The more you prepare before a formal RFP is issued, the better off you'll be. While you won't know about all RFPs before they're issued, your marketing and sales staff should be tracking potential clients and know when current supplier contracts are coming up for renewal or re-bid.

Most formal RFPs include limitations on contact with the client and their staff once the RFP is issued, which limits your ability to gather information that can be useful to your proposal response. In many cases, making unauthorized contact with the client during an RFP process can get you disqualified from bidding.

For less formal or non-competitive proposal submissions, this will be less of an issue, but making contact during the process is risky. It's better to start preparing in advance if you know about an upcoming RFP.

For formal RFPs, you can use the pre-RFP issue phase to make contact with individuals in the organization, gather more information, or introduce key individuals from your company to the organization. This makes it easier for you to respond to the proposal once it's issued, and the client will have more of a connection with the people in your company.

Another advantage to engaging clients before the RFP is released is to educate them on other issues and considerations related to the service, and give them ideas and information they could include in the RFP itself. This can include building in requirements you can easily meet, additional services you can provide, specifications you already work with or criteria that match your capabilities.

While sharing information and making introductions is valuable, you can also use the pre-RFP period to do more research on the issues, the client and the service and, if relevant, align yourself with the right subcontractors, service providers and even technical or writing assistance for the proposal itself. The more of this you do in advance, the more time you can spend during the RFP phase on your proposal response strategy and the crafting of an effective written proposal.

2. RFP review

Once you receive the RFP documentation, carefully review the entire RFP to prepare for developing the response, and to identify issues, concerns or details that will impact your proposal.

While it depends on your services and the RFP itself, here are typical things you should look at to ensure you can prepare your proposal effectively. Sometimes simple things like missing a mandatory site visit, not having the insurance requirement in place, or other details will disqualify you.

Some of the things you should look for include:

- ☑ The RFP process.
- ☑ Overall timelines.
- ☑ Mandatory requirements.
- ☑ Scoring, evaluation criteria and weighting.
- ☑ Process for submitting questions, including deadlines.
- ☑ Sources of additional information, such as a data room or online source.
- ☑ Site tour dates and other client meetings.
- ☑ The actual scope of work.
- ☑ Specifications and service levels.
- ☑ Financial proposal submission requirements, forms, etc.
- ☑ Technical (written) proposal requirements.
- ☑ Submission (delivery) requirements.
- ☑ Insurance and bonding requirements.
- ☑ Minimum experience requirements.
- ☑ Page count, margins and type size requirements.

If the client provided a sample contract as part of the RFP, review it carefully to see what may impact your service solution or pricing. Some RFPs require you to accept their contract as-is while others invite comment and modification through a specific process. Use care when objecting to clauses in the contract. Be sure they really matter, otherwise you risk creating a negative impression by objecting to insignificant issues.

The information you must provide and the questions you must answer in response to the RFP proposal tell you what background information you need and the resources you require to address them effectively. This is the time to source those resources and set deadlines internally.

3. Strategy

A strategy is one of the most important things you need. Strategy sets the direction and provides you with the information and approach you need to manage and write a successful proposal. Much of this will stem from the proposal review process that you've undertaken.

One way to start this process is to hold a strategy session that includes key senior people, as well as a range of subject matter experts, operational staff, subcontractors, and anyone else who can provide input add value to your strategy.

Example

Using a strategy session:

For a non-profit organization submitting a proposal for funding, a focused strategy session helped them determine what the funding agency was looking for, who the evaluators would be, and what focus would maximize their chances of receiving funding.

Consider this part of the process ongoing. Set up several sessions during the process to reconfirm and incorporate new material and insight that may have been discovered along the way.

Your strategy includes a number of elements you need to take the time to assess and develop. This includes themes to use when writing your proposal, client hot buttons you need to address, and a gap-analysis. These strategic elements are discussed in more detail further below.

4. Kick-off

Getting everyone on the same page makes it easier to develop an effective proposal. A kick-off meeting gets a proposal project started by giving everyone the information they need, and confirming resources and priorities.

The kick-off meeting includes individuals from other departments who are involved in delivering the product or service, as well as subcontractors or other partners. You should also invite anyone who will be preparing material for your proposal. Don't limit these meetings to the senior people or heads of departments. Get frontline resources involved. They can often contribute the details and subtle information that will make your proposal more successful.

In the kick-off meeting, outline the results of your RFP review and any initial strategy you've developed. Provide the project plan and discuss information the group needs to know in order to help with the proposal.

At this meeting, clearly identify the responsibilities and timelines required for a successful proposal. Some of the individuals present may have already been included in the strategy sessions.

The Agenda should include the following elements:

- ☑ Review the technical proposal requirements (format, etc.) and establish action items if required.
- ☑ Review the proposal response content requirements, and determine the required proposal format, instructions to writers, etc.
- ☑ Discuss and assess the response areas to validate and communicate the related hot buttons, key messages and opportunities.

- ☑ Identify and assess potential internal and external resources who should be followed up to gain adequate information and nuances regarding client needs, expectations and agenda.
- ☑ Assign key research activities required, both to gain outside information, and for internal information required to respond to the proposal itself.
- ☑ Provide an initial 'straw-man' organization and solution for the proposal, including both staff and methodology for the service delivery model around which the proposal writers will frame their written material.
- ☑ Provide writing guidelines, styles, logistics, etc.
- ☑ Establish writing assignments.
- ☑ Generate an initial list of questions for the client.

5. Pricing

Although you need to clearly understand the pricing model, the client expects that as part of the proposal submission and you will provide it to them in the format and structure they require. However, you may want to propose an alternate model based on your own experience and advantages.

The pricing model in the RFP may be based on what the client feels comfortable with for best pricing, and so that the client can get information they can use for the negotiation process.

There may be better ways to handle pricing that reduces risk or makes service changes more flexible. In addition, if your product or service approach is different, there may be pricing models that make them more attractive.

By making an alternative proposal, and clearly identifying the reasons for it, as long as it isn't prohibited in the RFP, you could have the advantage. It's important, however, to provide pricing in accordance with RFP requirements to avoid being disqualified or disadvantaged. If a client doesn't get what they expect and can't compare you with others the way they expect, the client may not look favorably on your approach, even if you have a compelling reason for your alternate methods.

6. Service solution

Your service solution outlines how you're going to deliver the product or service, as well as the type and specifications of the product or the organizational structure and processes for the service. Knowing what the solution is at the beginning of the proposal process makes it easier to develop the written proposal response. Without it, your written response won't be as effective, or you will need to re-write some of it after you've finalized your solution.

The solution must effectively match the strategy, client needs and the compelling examples and explanation you will provide to demonstrate why your solution is the best.

Sometimes your solution will be developed in parallel with the writing. While this is far from ideal, if you have to do it this way, carefully manage the process so the right information is available for the written response when it is needed.

Lesson Learned

Putting the cart before the horse:

We were writing a proposal response for a service without knowing the final organizational structure or how the services would be delivered. Generic processes and information with placeholders were included in the proposal at first, which meant a re-write was necessary just before submission to align the writing with the final solution. This wasted effort, used up time we should have spent fine-tuning the response, and left room for errors.

To make an effective and compelling written proposal, you need to describe how the service will be delivered and why it matters to the client. This must be done at the beginning of the process to take full advantage of an effective proposal writing process.

While most RFPs require you to respond to requirements based on specific service levels and performance or technical specifications, some proposals will ask for service options and suggestions for efficiency and lower cost. This is your opportunity to provide alternatives that may be more attractive to the client, and make you more competitive.

If the client has not asked, and unless they specifically prohibit it, you should propose alternate service options that may be attractive to the client. There may be services they haven't considered, or a different way of providing the results they want. Do this in addition to the clients stated services and scope, with any related costing clearly identified as optional.

This can include a proposal for the basic requirements the client has asked for, as well as either an increase in scope, or absorbing other contracted services, for instance, which may enable you to provide more scope for less cost than the client spends on multiple providers. It may also be beneficial to propose a reduced scope that still meets the client's basic requirements, particularly if you know cost is an issue. Sometimes the requirements the client documents don't reflect real conditions. The more you know about the client's business, the better you'll be able to propose alternative service solutions.

7. Management solution

In addition to the service solution, provide a compelling management solution that goes beyond the technical approach to your service and meets or exceeds the client's requirements. Specifically address the customer/supplier relationship and how you will manage the service or product delivery over the life of the contract, including quality assurance, auditing, reporting, and client interfaces.

More extensive RFPs include questions that cover this are. If they do, put as much effort into answering them as you do for the service solution or pricing. The reason the client issued an RFP is to get the best solution, not just a price. How you manage the service is important to the overall solution.

Consider your technical solution and pricing approach in addition to your understanding of the client when developing the interfaces, management and reporting approaches and service management tools that will be part of your proposal. These must be of interest to the client and attract them to your overall solution.

For a service, particularly when it's a key support to the client's core business and success, the relationship, accessibility, culture, reporting, quality management and supplier relationship management approaches should be developed and proposed in a way that enhances your offering and provides benefits to the client.

8. Style sheet

Your style sheet provides information to your proposal contributors, and ensures consistent information, correct terminology, consistent use of titles, how and which acronyms are to be used, how to use headings and bullets, headings, naming of illustrations, and even instructs on the response's tone and approach.

This is particularly important with a large proposal where many different groups, internal or external, will be contributing to the RFP response.

By using a style sheet, you reduce errors, provide a more cohesive proposal to the client, and save a lot of time at the end of the process when you are under pressure to finalize the proposal.

The style sheet should be accompanied by a copy of the template document, to be used by everybody writing the proposal. A template saves time, energy, and reduces errors. It ensures your contributors are developing consistent material using the same format and structure. It will mean less work and less time consolidating the various contributions to the proposal.

The style sheet should include the following key elements:

- ☑ Basic background information on the client and the overall scope.
- ☑ Document and file naming and numbering conventions.

- ☑ Writing techniques to be used, such as when to expand acronyms, use of headings, formatting of information, etc.
- ☑ How to refer to the client and your company in the written response.
- ☑ Descriptions of the solutions that are important when writing, including processes, names of systems and products, responsibilities, org charts, titles, etc.
- ☑ Client's terminology, acronyms, position titles and other information that needs to be referred to accurately and consistently throughout the proposal.
- ☑ Terminology or issues that should not be discussed or used due to sensitivities or interpretations by the client.
- ☑ Key elements to include in each section or to be answered in questions, such as benefits, examples, process diagrams, etc., to maintain consistency.
- ☑ Hot buttons and issues that should be covered in each section where possible.
- ☑ Format and naming/reference conventions, as well as the format of attachments, images, diagrams and screen shots used in the proposal.

The size and complexity of your RFP response will dictate how much information you need to include in your style sheet, as will your approach to the writing exercise and the resources you have available. Even if you use dedicated writers or editors to help you with your proposal, you will save time and effort by having the source material developed using the style sheet.

9. Project plan

No matter how small or large your proposal response will be, you need a project plan with your resources, schedule and tasks identified to ensure you get to the final submission date with a finished proposal.

The larger and more complex the proposal, the more critical is your plan and the more detailed it should be. Proposals can range from less than 25 pages to over 1,000 pages, depending on the client's scope and requirements, as well as their approach to the RFP process.

Your general plan can be developed during the pre-RFP release phase, but it's usually refined and developed around the RFP milestones such as site visits, Q&A dates and the final submission date.

The plan helps you identify the resources you need and, more importantly, the decision-making required and potential bottlenecks within your organization. Clearly identify internal and external resources and when their involvement or submissions are required.

Large projects that are a considerable commitment or risk to your company may require multiple hurdles and sign-offs within your organization, including financial, legal, risk management and production or operations. Make sure you understand these hurdles, are well prepared for them, and build them into your schedule.

This part of the process is basically project management. Your success depends on careful management of resources and timelines to keep work on track and in the correct order to meet the deadlines and submit your proposal on time. Never rely on a delay or extension. Asking for an extension can send a bad signal to your potential client.

The resources you identify should be the ones who can deliver what you need. In any organization, it may be difficult to find subject matter experts who are also good at writing. It can be easier to pair up these staff with someone else who understands the business area and can write, rather than try to work with someone who is either incapable or uncomfortable with the formal task of writing.

The schedule is important to a successful proposal, especially for a large, complicated RFP response. You can manage the schedule yourself, or assign an assistant to manage it for you. Like project management, this requires a detail-oriented individual with a strong personality to ensure the work gets done on time.

Your proposal response plan should include:

- ☑ All resources needed to complete the proposal response.
- ☑ Timelines and due-dates for all parts of the process, including internal approvals.
- ☑ A process for updating and monitoring progress.
- ☑ Meetings and internal review dates during the process.
- ☑ Logistics (records management and documentation control).
- ☑ Identification of an individual who will provide control and management of the various parts of the proposal.
- ☑ Identification of individuals and their specific tasks or assignments.

10. Version control

For a proposal with multiple contributors, maintaining control over documents and revisions will prevent mistakes and wasted effort during the writing, editing and review process.

Use a central approach with a file numbering and naming convention. The filename structure will help you manage the information, consolidate the final proposal, and find information. Since most large proposals are developed in parts that are eventually assembled together, this will save you time and effort at the end.

Your filename structure should include the following information:

Format:

Project Name – Section – Type – (Date).doc

Example:

ApexLogistics – HR 3.2 – Main Body (10.03.23).doc

- **Project Name**: The name of the project, often the name or acronym used by the client.

- **Section**: The section description in the RFP document. This may be numerical based on the RFP numbering, or a descriptive title such as Mandatory, Human Resources, Information Technology, Organization, Quality Assurance, etc.
- **Type:** Indicates what the document is for. It may be the main body, attachment, illustration or picture, or even unedited source material, such as resumes that are being shortened down to half-a-page for eventual inclusion in the main body. Use a simple naming convention.
- **Date:** The date the document was last changed. Don't rely on the file name dates. Every time a file is edited, save it with the current date at the end of the filename. While this may result in a lot of files, it provides useful backups and enables you to go back to previous versions if necessary.

If multiple people work on the same files, have them add their initials in the filename. Part of the control process should be to ensure only one individual is working on a file at a given time.

In addition, use the tools available in Word Processors such as MS Word® to track changes. This allows you to see what changes are made, and to accept or reject changes.

Part of this process should include backing up on a regular basis and checking for viruses. Be especially cautious if contributors are working on these files at a subcontractor's office or at home on their own computers. The amount of effort that goes into the written response can be immense, and the last thing you want to do is lose something because of a virus or computer crash.

11. Iteration and consolidation

With a large proposal, multiple contributors and many sections, the only manageable process is with multiple files, but ultimately the files will need to be consolidated

This involves putting all the separate parts together in one document, and verifying page count, facilitating an overall review, and ensuring consistency, headings and the table of content.

If you've used a template for all contributions, this will be as simple as cutting and pasting all the parts into a single document, or using the word processor's merging capabilities. With a template and consistent styles and formatting, this will be easy. Otherwise, be prepared for a lot of extra effort to fix the formatting inconsistencies and other errors.

12. Production and delivery

Even for small projects, production and delivery need to be accounted for in the project plan, whether the proposal is to be delivered by courier or by hand. Either way, it's important to make sure the response gets to the destination on time. Investigate courier pick-up times and guaranteed delivery schedules, or how much time it takes to hand-deliver, including making sure whoever is delivering the proposal knows how to get to the client's office. In any case, build in some buffer time to accommodate delays or issues. If you hand-deliver the proposal, get a receipt of some kind to prove it was delivered on time.

Production of a large proposal can take a considerable amount of time. While some things can be prepared ahead of time, such as binder covers, divider tabs etc., the rest of the proposal can only be produced and packaged after you've completed a final version.

If possible, have a least one copy produced for review before you have multiple copies produced. This gives lets you review the proposal in its final format and make changes as required.

While one of the easiest solutions is outsourcing this work to a print shop, you can sometimes have more control in-house if you have the resources and the time. If you outsource this to a print shop, be sure you have a strong working relationship with the print shop, and that they recognize the critical importance of on-time delivery. Check whether the print shop is willing to stay open after hours to meet your deadlines.

Your production will be based on the RFP submission requirements, which may outline the format, sections, number of copies (including the number of originals), and how they're labeled. Follow these instructions carefully, but in addition, make sure your documents are easy to use and it's easy to find the sections. If you're producing a large technical response, you could, for example, consider including a quick reference guide that includes a list of acronyms on one side and a list of sections on the other.

Manage the Process, Don't Let it Manage You

Whether you're writing a large or small proposal response, take control of the process so that everything that goes into developing, writing and producing the proposal is managed on a timely basis, not only to meet deadlines, but also to ensure the process doesn't take up an unnecessary amount of your time.

Take an aggressive project management approach by starting with a plan and managing to that plan. This way, you can focus your attention on the strategic aspects of the proposal, and put together a persuasive proposal you can deliver on time. This is even more important for large complex proposals that require input from various contributors and subject matter experts, operational groups, corporate groups or subcontractors.

Surviving the Site Tour and Bidders Meetings

If you've gone on tours and attended bidders meetings, you may wonder about their value. Seldom does anyone ask good questions, and the information you gather isn't usually critical to the bid. Very few bidders want to ask key questions when they know they'll either reveal their lack of knowledge, or give their competitors information that may help them.

Of course, that depends on how much you already know and how familiar you are with the client's needs. If you look at the site tours and bidder meetings as a strategic opportunity to collect information you can use, you'll be able to get value.

Whether the meetings or tours are mandatory or not, send someone from your organization. Sometimes, the client uses the tours as an opportunity to share important information, but you may not know that in advance. Attendance also demonstrates your interest in the client and respect for the process.

Who you send will depend on the event. If senior level clients will be present, send your senior level staff. If a site tour is hosted by the local manager, send someone who is experienced in details and knows what to look for.

There are several approaches to getting value from site tours and bidders meetings. The key requirement is to prepare the individuals attending so they can actually add value to your proposal writing process. The individual attending needs to understand the scope, the client, your possible solution and issues you may be interested in, usually gathered at your strategic planning. You may even need to tell the individual attending what to look for, and ensure they take notes.

Bidders meeting

- Listen very carefully to the terms and phrases the client uses and write them down. These can be used in your proposal to reflect back to the client, as discussed in Part 6.
- You don't have to ask questions during the meetings. Write down questions for submission later during the formal Q&A process.
- Engage the client. Be visible and talk to them before and after the formal portion of the meeting. Look directly at them while they deliver their presentation to make eye contact, and nod your head or use other facial cues to show you're listening.

Site tours

- A good, informal way of gathering information during a site visit is to identify the client personnel and the main client contact. Introduce yourself and engage in conversation. Make comments and observations to gauge their reaction, show your interest and demonstrate what you know. Depending on the client and the nature of the procurement rules, ask questions with caution, but respect their choice to not answer. Don't press the point.

- Look for facts and details you can include in the proposal. This is not restricted to information that helps you develop your bid. It can be as simple as noting whether the client has a newsletter, or whether they have information about a help desk number, or slogans or initiatives they may be promoting with posters or notices. These details may help you with further research, help you link your solution with something the client is doing, or simply allow you to later refer to something the client considers important.
- If you don't already know the competitors, introduce yourself to each one and engage in discussion. While this may seem to be about revealing yourself, if you do it right, you'll learn more than they will. Sometimes you can learn whom your competition is partnering or subcontracting with. This information can be used effectively when ghosting your competition, a technique discussed in Part 5.

Herding Cats

Part of the process includes gathering input and written elements from other individuals and organizations, including internal and subcontracted or partner organizations.

If you're managing proposals, you probably know what happens when you're looking for staff within your operations and corporate groups to help with a proposal. Suddenly, people are very hard to find, and so overwhelmed with work that they can't possibly help you.

Unfortunately, you may be one of the few individuals who really cares about submitting the proposal on time and in a format and structure that will ensure you win.

In most cases the individuals to whom you're turning to for contributions have day jobs. In addition, they often don't have a stake in the proposal's success. As a result, you will end up chasing them to get what you need, and you'll need it to finish the proposal on time.

You can encourage more active involvement and access to these individuals by ensuring their managers understand the importance of the proposal and their staff's contribution. Make the proposal highly visible and have your own senior managers or even the president identify the importance.

By having the request come from the top instead of sideways you should get the attention of these individuals and improve their participation. By adding them to the project plan and identifying due dates, you'll have a visible way to encourage on-time participation.

If you need to, copy their boss on correspondence, due dates and other key information, including thanking them for their contribution. It's not that the individuals don't care, it's just that their priorities are not always the same as yours. Your best defense is to understand this will happen and guard against it.

Pulling Teeth

Even with cooperative resources, getting individuals to contribute in a meaningful way can be challenging.

There are two ways to address this. First, make it as easy and painless as possible for individuals to contribute. For some people, this simply means not making them do the actual writing. For others, it's by being very specific about what you're asking for so they don't need to guess, and aren't at risk of doing the wrong thing. Like everything, cooperation has a lot to do with understanding people, their motivations and individual personalities.

For anybody who doesn't like to write, simply asking them to jot down information that you or somebody else can then craft into proper written text will accomplish what you really need – information and ideas from somebody who knows something about the subject.

A good way to do this is with a simple form. You can use the template information described below. The actual questions you ask will need to match the proposal requirements and the nature of the questions themselves, but the list below gives you an idea. Some of the questions could potentially become headings in the proposal response.

- ☑ Original question from RFP.
- ☑ Short list of hot buttons and solutions you think you need to provide to the client in order to win.
- ☑ The following questions (indicating to the expert that a point form response is acceptable):
    - Why is this solution, method or product valuable?
    - What are the key features that meet client requirements?
    - Where has this been done before successfully?
    - What would be the key steps to implementation?
    - What would be the ongoing interaction and communication with the client after implementation?
    - What information or results, including reporting, can be provided to the client? Provide samples.
    - What analysis and decision-making can come from this information that might be valuable to the client?
    - The client may be concerned with XXX – how would you address this?
    - Are there any existing documents, which could help respond to this question? (Policies and procedures, process diagrams, training material, etc.)

Use a variation of this checklist to suit your specific needs with either your own staff within particular subject matter areas, or with subcontractors providing a specific service as part of a bundled product or service delivery. You will get more consistent results and address the key points you need to include in the proposal in order to be persuasive.

Simply asking experts to write something for you on a particular topic, or giving them a question posed in the RFP and asking them to respond to it will give you very inconsistent results. Most likely you will need to go back to the individuals for clarification and additional information in order to successfully structure the response and meet your messaging goals.

Reality Check – The Red Team

When working on a proposal, you get to the point where you're so invested in your material that it's hard to see the forest through the trees. This is when you need a Reality Check.

An internal review during the development process keeps you on-track and provides another viewpoint – one that is closer to the client than you. This internal review is often called the "Red Team," since the reviewers wield their red pens to mark up your proposal.

To get the best value, you need to pick reviewers who will be able to deliver critical and thoughtful input. You aren't looking for people who will focus on punctuation and grammar. You need people who can understand the evaluation criteria, and provide comments on where you hit the mark and, most importantly, where you don't.

In addition to choosing the right people for the Red Team, you need to prepare them with background material, and let them know what you need and how you'll use their input.

To make the review process more effective, provide the team with specific guidance before asking them to review the material. This way, you'll have them looking at the proposal response from the client perspective, based on the strategy you've established.

The Red Team needs to be supplied with the style sheet, which talks about the themes, hot buttons and other key elements of your proposal approach, so they can compare your proposal with your intent. They also need to be provided with the scoring matrix the client will use to evaluate your proposal, if it was provided.

If it wasn't provided in the RFP, you need to take your best guess about what the client will be looking for and provide the Red Team with that. Using the scoring matrix gives the reviewers an opportunity to rate your proposal and mark it up with comments.

By preparing the reviewers well, they'll be able to focus on the content in a way that lines up with what the client is likely to be looking for, rather than focusing on minor items. While you should welcome the reviewers' spelling and grammar edits, make their real purpose and value clear to them so you get what you need out of the exercise.

The best approach is to provide the documentation to the Red Team reviewers so they can make notes and mark up the document itself. If you have a large proposal, you may need to split it up and have several people review different sections. When possible, have more than one person review each part of your proposal.

Lessons Learned

Pick your Red Team wisely and tell them what you want:

Some members of a Red Team, including senior managers, spent most of the review correcting grammar and spelling. Their input would have been more valuable for pointing out inconsistencies, and missed opportunities to focus on the message, hot buttons, value, competitive advantage, etc.

Once the individual reviewers have gone over the document, get together as a group. If the reviewers review the document as a group first, there will be too much discussion about various points, and not enough focus on what you want them to be doing for you.

It's very important that key elements of your proposal, such as the strategy and technical solution, are decided before the review process is undertaken. Establishing these elements is not the purpose of the Red Team review.

Keep a tight rein on the group to ensure you're getting the value you need out of the meeting and the contributions. Side discussion and tangential issues should be quickly refocused on whether the client's question has been answered in a compelling manner that will receive a high evaluation and get you to the table with the client.

Depending on the size and importance of the proposal, you may want to do this process twice, first with the draft material, and then with a follow-up after you've re-edited the material and taken into account the first review. You can use the same reviewers, different reviewers or a mix of the two. The second round should be even more focused – ensuring that the message is clear and evident.

Who you select for the review team is important. The makeup of the review team shouldn't just be senior people, it should be subject matter experts and operation staff who will provide valuable, useful input on what you need to change to make your proposal response more relevant.

You can also make the review process more informal by having other people within your organization review and comment on parts of the proposal with which they haven't been involved. This fresh view may reveal issues that only someone who is not involved can identify.

Example

Getting a high-level review:

In a large organization, proposals were considered so important that the president himself reviewed all major proposals, and provided comments and suggestions for improvement.

Your Proposal Team

If you're fortunate to have a team to produce and write proposal responses, it's useful to understand the various roles that may be required. If you're alone or have a very small team, possibly even borrowed resources put together solely for the proposal response, it will help to have a picture of the overall responsibilities and how to divide the work.

With a larger team, the responsibilities will be spread over more people with more focused responsibilities. Obviously in a smaller team many of these roles will be combined.

Proposal manager

The proposal manager is essentially the director of the orchestra. Whether this is you or someone else, the proposal manager coordinates resources and tasks, ensures things are being done on time, and reports up the chain of command to senior executives responsible for proposals or the particular line of business the proposal is about.

A proposal manager needs to be detail-oriented and have superior project management skills. They should also be creative and strategic thinkers. They don't necessarily need to be great writers if there are other contributors. Marketing and sales skills are useful, but not critical.

The larger your team, the more you should rely on other individuals for specialized responsibilities and skills. It's very rare to find all of these attributes in one individual.

Proposal administrator

The proposal administrator works with the proposal manager to keep track of details. They ensure you adequately deal with all of the mandatory requirements, and facilitate tasks within the organization on behalf of the proposal manager.

These include maintaining the schedule, distribution lists and various communications to other team members and individuals within the organization who may not be part of the core proposal team, but are helping with the response, including subcontractors and the suppliers who are involved. An important task is tracking deliverables and following up to ensure on-time receipt of information, materials and decisions from others within the company.

Sales and marketing manager

This is the person with the sales and marketing experience. They're the ones who develop unique selling points, features and benefits in addition to teasing out the phrasing, terminology, hot buttons, themes and other elements for the proposal. This individual needs to have sales and marketing expertise and be very creative. They should also be able to work closely with the subject matter experts and the business leaders to ensure the sales and marketing pitch is grounded in the solution, not just presented as empty marketing material.

Financial or pricing manager

This individual may be part of your existing financial team. They're the ones who will take the information from the proposal manager and sales manager to help develop pricing for the proposal.

The financial/pricing manager must understand the cost inputs and financial issues for the proposed service, and be involved in establishing margins and profits, factoring in many of the other expenses that are often hidden but will result from new business. In addition to their expertise with numbers, the financial/pricing manager will act as a counterpoint to the salespeople and proposal manager. The sales and proposal manager's primary responsibility and goal is to win the proposal, the financial/pricing manager needs to ensure it’s on reasonable financial terms, based on the chosen strategy for pricing in the particular market.

Proposal writer

The proposal writer crafts the final text for your proposal. Preferably, they will have some background and experience related to the products and services you sell. If they don't, you need to give them a quick education by having them discuss these products and services with line managers, salespeople and others within your organization. The more they understand what they're writing about, the more they will be able to write effectively. After all, writing a proposal isn't just about the words, it's about the product or service.

Copy editor

The copy editor comes in near the end of the process and will go through the proposal with a fine-tooth comb, correcting spelling and grammar, punctuation and other issues, including consistency of terminology, titles, etc.

This is a very specific skill that requires not only excellent knowledge of spelling, grammar and punctuation, but also an attention to detail. It's important that this individual is not involved with the writing itself. If you have the financial resources, hire a professional. If not, find one or more people within your organization who are good at editing, and get them to edit the final proposal document.

Summary

Writing a proposal, particularly a large one, is a long, tedious task. You need good planning, management and shepherding of resources, and a good understanding of the stages and processes. You need to review the RFP and develop your strategy and establish your pricing, technical and management solutions before you begin writing your proposal.

Techniques You Can Use:

- ✓ Managing a proposal is similar to managing a project.
- ✓ Before you start writing, set the foundation for your response.
- ✓ Develop your plan, establish the resources, and get help.
- ✓ Understand the purpose of your response (RFI, RFQ, RFP, etc.) and write your response accordingly.

Traps To Avoid:

- ✖ Don't start writing before you know your strategy and solution.
- ✖ Don't make it hard for other contributors to help.
- ✖ Don't solicit resources without support from above.

Your Action Plan to Write Better Proposals:

Based on this chapter, list several things you need to do or must do differently to win more business with your proposals.

Priority	Things to Do

Part 3
Prepare for Battle – Strategy for Success

A proposal is about winning against your competition. A winning strategy includes planning your approach, understanding the client and your competition, and developing and presenting your messages and supporting evidence in a way that convinces the client to select your bid.

By taking a strategic rather than a tactical approach, you are more likely to hit the mark with the client and produce a persuasive proposal.

Effective strategic techniques discussed in this section include:

- Understanding the requirements goes beyond reading the RFP.
- Focus on the evaluation process and the evaluators themselves.
- Overcome limitations and weaknesses offensively.

> *"Strategy without tactics is the slowest route to victory. Tactics without strategy is the noise before defeat."*
>
> *– Sun Tzu, Chinese General*

It's More Than Just Writing a Proposal

Successfully responding to a proposal is about more than just writing material. A common error is to simply start writing based on the response requirements of the RFP. You need a real strategy to be successful, a strategy based on many factors, not just what is written in the RFP or based on informal discussions.

Example

The RFP doesn't always spell out everything you need to know:

While responding to an RFP for a government organization where the RFP requirements were very lean on detail, research revealed a report to the board of directors containing plans for the RFP that outlined considerably more detail and the rationale for the RFP. This helped formulate the response and allowed for incorporation of details that other competitors may not have included.

Letting your subject matter experts, or even worse, professional writers or marketing staff, simply put words on paper without a strategy to guide them, is a recipe for failure.

Before anybody starts writing, you need to establish a strategic approach to the proposal response. This will include the key messages that you want to put forward. The strategy will be developed and the messages identified based on careful analysis and research. Whether you dig deeply or not, this approach to winning proposals will give you the advantage over your competition.

Develop Your Response Strategy

Developing a strategy for your response is one of the most important things you'll do. Simply putting words on paper won't get the attention you need to win proposals.

What does the client want?

This isn't always what it seems. What the client says in the proposal and what they may have said in public statements may be somewhat different from what they really want from the RFP. You need to read between the lines and use other sources to find out exactly what's important to them client. For instance, the client frequently states that price is not necessarily the deciding factor. You can be assured, however, that price will be a key factor and will almost always influence the decision. With this in mind, for instance, you can structure your proposal with optional services and alternative pricing structures to meet the client's needs. Other information you find about the client and what they really want or need can be used in your proposal to develop a response that is more effective than the competition's.

Themes

The purpose of establishing themes is to ensure your message is delivered within each question you're responding to in the RFP.

Themes are compelling messages you want to continually put in front of the client while they're reading the proposal. It's like running repetitive advertisements to get better exposure for your product or service. The real strategy is to ensure the client remembers the messages when they're scoring your proposal.

Themes also help anyone writing material for you, whether they're staff or subcontractors, to understand what your main message is and hopefully see ways to incorporate it into their contribution, making the overall process easier for you while also strengthening the proposal.

Themes are things that provide support to your overall proposal, show your benefit or competitive advantage, or are important to the client. They demonstrate why the client should select you, and should be directly related to client issues, needs or expectations.

The themes should be woven throughout your entire proposal. Depending on what they are, you can simply write them into the text, or add a separate heading within each section or question to focus on that theme.

Example	**Your theme is a consistent message about what the client cares about:** If, for example, Information Technology, data and reporting are important to the client, add a heading in each section to explain how your solution deals with the topic and benefits the client. Use the same approach for anything else that is key to winning your bid.

Develop your themes during your strategic planning and strategy sessions. The information in the RFP documents and what the client has told you are only two sources for effective themes. You must look at the client's business, the history of the current service contract, news releases, annual reports, industry issues and your competitors. Get insight from your staff and, where possible, contacts who used to work for the client or even the incumbent, if possible.

Hot buttons

Hot buttons are the most pressing and important issues facing the client. You may not be able to identify them from reading the RFP or from listening to what the client tells you. Like themes, identifying hot buttons requires research.

Hot buttons are different than themes. While themes are overall issues you typically repeat throughout your proposal, hot buttons are usually single-issue items that are dealt with in specific parts of the proposal response.

You will win more business by showing you understand the client's key issues and by demonstrating how you support the client's issues or can mitigate them with your service or product solution

The hot buttons aren't always directly related to the requirements of the RFP. They may be something else you've learned about the client that really matters to them. If so, you can discuss that in your proposal, demonstrating your understanding of the client and the advantages you can provide.

Example

Understand the client's hot buttons:

If accountability legislation for public companies is a hot button for the client and they must adhere to it, you should clearly identify what you're doing within your organization that will support the client's requirements, or show that you're in compliance with the same requirement.

A hot button can be either something the client wants or needs and is interested in, or something the client badly wants to avoid.

Example

General industry hot buttons are also important:

Environmental issues are one of the timely hot buttons of interest to many clients. Clients may be fighting negative press about their environmental record, or striving to lead the industry with green initiatives. Either way, if you can emphasize how you can help, you will be hitting the client's hot button.

Once you've identified the hot buttons and how you plan to address them within your proposal response, list them on a checklist to make sure you address all of them.

Similar to other important information within your RFP document, make sure that when you're addressing a hot button issue, it's clear within your proposal response. Don't bury it with other material or hide it in long paragraphs. Use a heading, breakout box or other technique to direct the client's attention towards it. Use the techniques discussed in Part 7 to highlight how you address hot button issues.

Messages

Your proposal response strategy should include key messages that gain support from reviewers, points in the evaluation, and win the proposal.

These messages are not the same as themes, although themes should also be delivering a message. While the theme is something you can reuse throughout the entire proposal response, a message is often a specific, important item that addresses the requirements. Messages are dealt with in specific sections or as answers to specific questions. Messages present or position your company's offerings. They are also different from hot buttons, which are typically high profile items that have a big impact on the client.

Messages may include things the client doesn't even realize are important, but most often they're geared to the evaluation scoring and your competitive advantages.

These messages may include:

- ☑ The level of skills and experience of your staff.
- ☑ How you bring improvement to clients.
- ☑ The benefits of your product or service.
- ☑ How a transition to your company will be seamless.
- ☑ Your advantages over the competition.
- ☑ Your knowledge and understanding of the client's requirements.
- ☑ Your success in achieving the performance requirements or service levels the client is expecting.

You develop your messages during the planning and strategy session based on the client's needs and your solution. During this process, you identify things that matter to the client. Develop these into a consistent yet concise message that is crafted to get the attention of the evaluators and get the most evaluation points.

Key attributes of your message should be:

- ✓ Impact
- ✓ Relevance
- ✓ Support for your proposal

Each of your messages has to be supported with facts and information and cannot just be presented as typical marketing and sales language. Some of the techniques are discussed in Part 6.

Negate concerns

The biggest mistake you can make is pretending negative issues or concerns the client may have about your firm don't exist.

No matter how much you think your company and your product or service is superior, you can assume there are people who don't agree. Unfortunately, some of these people may be evaluating your proposal.

You must always consider what these concerns could be and negate them. When presenting to an audience, you have the ability to defend your statements and positions when objections are raised. In a proposal, you only have one opportunity – when you write it.

Even industry perceptions and rumors can be damaging.

Tip | The law of candor is the 15th law of marketing in *The 22 Immutable Laws of Marketing* by Al Ries and Jack Trout. The authors explain that an effective way of getting a positive reaction is to admit a negative attribute and turn it into a positive.

By identifying these concerns, and putting them up front and center and dealing with them, you'll ensure that client perceptions will be managed and you'll be able to get your message across rather than having the client's negative assumptions prevail.

Some of these negative issues will come out of your strategic analysis and you can use those findings to address the negative concerns. Others may be harder to find. Individuals in your organization may have heard things from contacts within the industry and even the client, but haven't brought them to your attention. Seek out honest and frank opinions and observations from others. Hearing them may not be enjoyable, but not addressing them may lose business.

Other issues will be fairly obvious. You may be a new entrant into the marketplace and have some very specific disadvantages. If you're generally more expensive, that could also be negative. If you lost a rebid or renewal recently, perhaps even with a competitor on this RFP, it will raise questions about why you lost the business. Always assume the perception will be negative, and find a way to deal with it.

Tip

In *Yes!: 50 Scientifically Ways to Be Persuasive*, the authors outline a number of high-profile examples, including a study by Kip Williams, a social psychologist. Williams's study revealed that juries were more likely to be favorable of the defendant if their lawyers raised minor weaknesses in the case before the prosecution did.

Sometimes, you can find a negative issue or even what may seem like a competitive disadvantage and explain to the client why it isn't negative at all. Even if you don't fully convince the client, raising and acknowledging a negative issue the client is probably already aware of will make you appear more trustworthy.

Addressing the evaluation criteria

When responding to an RFP, your goal is to get the highest possible evaluation score. Typically the proposal response scoring will be weighted with financial, technical and other criteria.

The technical portion of the RFP is usually the written response to questions with your solution, background and other information about how you would fulfill the requirements. Within this part of the RFP, scoring is usually further divided between sections such as Human Resources (HR), technology, implementation, previous experience, approach to various services, and more.

Within each of these sections there are questions the client wants you to answer so they can evaluate your response. In some cases, the individual questions will also have a weighting attached to them, but in most cases there's no indication of what's more important to the client.

In addition to the scoring matrix, the client may develop evaluation criteria. The criteria describe in words what they're looking for and what's important to them. How this criteria is presented in the RFP can vary widely and may not be made public.

Example

Examples of evaluation criteria include:

"Does the approach take into consideration the specific requirements of the RFP?

"Does their experience demonstrate that they have worked in the same environment as our requirements?"

"Have they answered the question completely?"

"Are examples provided that demonstrate existing processes are in place?"

"Is the response compliant with the specification requirements?"

In many cases the evaluators will have a checklist that emulates the evaluation scoring questions in the RFP, and they may score each of the questions on a scale of 1 to 5 or a percentage rating.

The evaluation process is tedious and time-consuming, so the easier you make it for the evaluators, the more likely it is that they will be able to understand your message and give you a high mark.

Look at the wording of the evaluation criteria and ensure you take that into consideration when responding. The art of responding to a proposal isn't simply a matter of telling the client what you'll do for them. You must frame it so evaluators will clearly see and evaluate you on your merits. Do this by emphasizing the characteristics of your proposal that match the characteristics of the evaluation criteria.

When you have others, including subcontractors or staff, writing for you, you need to provide them with the scoring matrix and evaluation criteria so they can incorporate it into their rough submission.

Evaluators have a tough job. They have to read large volumes of proposal responses that are often densely written and filled with fluff. They need to find evidence and information within the responses that match the questions asked and the evaluation criteria, then they need to decide what score to assign. Make this task as easy as possible.

Knowing and understanding the evaluators

Since winning proposals is about getting a high evaluation, it's useful to know more about the evaluators themselves.

By understanding who they are and what their interests are, you can speak to them directly in your proposal. Ensure you've taken into account any possible considerations, issues and sensitivities related to the service requirements. This generates a favorable response and a higher score based on evaluation criteria.

Unfortunately, the evaluation team composition is seldom identified in the RFP document. This is another example of an area you should be exploring before the RFP comes out if you're aware of it in advance. Even after the RFP comes out there may be avenues you can take to find out the makeup of the evaluation team. If you've worked with the client before, you may have an idea of how they compose their evaluation team, or you may know someone who has worked there in the past and can provide guidance.

You can also take an educated guess about what departments or groups from the client may be involved in addition to the procurement team. It doesn't need to be the exact individuals. For instance, for a service-related proposal that includes IT components, the IT department may be involved in addition to the operational or production department that the service will be provided to.

There may also be a quality assurance person or other client resources. Sometimes, the type and nature of the questions can provide clues about the evaluators.

Taking quality assurance as an example, if the client has a department or resource dedicated to the function, it's likely they will be called upon to evaluate anything directly related to quality assurance. As a result, it's important to directly speak to the quality assurance issues in a way that has credibility with the client's own expert and avoids general marketing claims.

This approach ensures that the things the evaluators are looking for are clearly seen and easily scored.

Regardless of how much information you're actually able to get on the evaluators, you need to make an effort to understand where they might be coming from so you can craft your response with that in mind. By using a more broadly-based approach and understanding what functional areas may be involved, you should be able to craft your responses to address the evaluators.

Lessons Learned

Knowing who will evaluate the RFP:

For an RFP response, it was obvious that the services would have a large impact on a particular operating unit within the client organization. Because members of the RFP response team had previously worked with the client, they were able to identify issues the client's staff would be concerned about and address these directly within the proposal.

If you're preparing an informal proposal without a formal structured evaluation team then you should already understand the client who is going to evaluate. In this case, your job is easier because instead of several evaluators who may have different or competing interests, you have a single audience.

If you haven't already learned enough about the evaluator, now is the time to do additional research to uncover their sensitivities. Some of the best sources are previous employees of the company who have interacted with the individuals or worked in their departments. You can often learn about individuals if they have a presence online.

Useful information includes previous seminars or speeches they have given, articles or associations they're involved in, press releases or projects they work on which have appeared in published material now available on the Internet. Read these carefully to gain a deeper understanding of their history and interests, and use them in concert with other techniques.

Example

Using the evaluator's background:

The key client representative for an RFP was very involved in an association related to the particular industry. The online information about the individual, including news articles with their quotes, committees they were involved with and focus of the association activities, helped identify things the individual would be interested in hearing about within the proposal response.

Questions to ask yourself

Part of a successful strategy, in addition to the items already discussed, is asking yourself questions about the client and the proposal. Asking questions is always an easy way to gather information, since the questions force you to examine issues and information.

The answers will guide you in your strategy and, most importantly, in determining what details and information to include in the proposal response.

Don't just ask one set of questions, however. After the first answer, ask more questions until you have good, quality information you can use in the proposal. At the least, you will know what answers you still don't have and need to investigate.

Some of the questions you should ask include the following:

- ☑ Why are they issuing an RFP now?
- ☑ Who will be reviewing?
- ☑ What is the selection process?
- ☑ What do they need?
- ☑ Who is doing the work now?
- ☑ Do they want change?
- ☑ How are they organized?
- ☑ Who will manage the contract?
- ☑ Who are their clients/customers?
- ☑ What is their core business?

Depending on the proposal and your situation, there may be additional questions you should be asking.

Once you've answered this first set of questions, ask more questions about the answer. For instance, after answering "Who will be reviewing?" you should ask "What are their interests?" Once you answer that, you should ask yourself "How can I incorporate that into the response?"

If You Aren't Sure, Ask

A common mistake is not asking questions when you're uncertain about how to address a particular question or requirement in the RFP, or how to respond to it effectively.

A normal concern is that by asking a question that the client sees as being obvious or simplistic, you'll seem as though you don't have the experience or expertise.

The other fear is that the answer from the client will also provide competitors with an advantage because most of the time, answers are provided to all bidders. While this may be true for some things, if you're truly uncertain or there's ambiguity about how to answer a question, asking for clarification may benefit your competitors. If you have confidence that you can respond more effectively than your competitor, you'll end up with the advantage, however. Otherwise you're simply guessing. If you guess right you'll do well, if you guess wrong you won't, but do you want to take the risk?

In this situation, a well-crafted question that appears to be helping the client looks good and gets the best possible response .

There's another approach you can use when it appears there's a mistake in the RFP itself. If allowed, contact the RFP's designated contact directly instead of using the formal question-and-answer process. The contact will be grateful you brought the error to their attention so they can issue an addendum or clarification. The exception to this approach is when you know how to interpret or deal with the error or mistake in the RFP document. In that case, there's very little advantage to raising the issue and having it clarified for your competition.

Dissecting the RFP

A formal RFP usually contains fairly typical requirements. The details will often depend on whether it's a government organization, public institution, public or private company, and how large and sophisticated the client is with their procurement approach. Typically, large sophisticated companies and government use very formal and rigid procurement practices to ensure fairness and visibility into the process . Others will have less rigid or formal approaches, but may still use well-defined evaluation criteria.

The RFP should identify the processes and timelines, including questions and answers, site visits, due dates, procurement rules, whether there will be oral presentations from bidders, evaluation processes, format, delivery instructions, and more.

Mandatory items

Most RFPs have mandatory requirements. This is often straightforward template-style material such as forms, declarations and documents, rather than a written response.

The mandatory requirements may involve a bid bond, conflict of interest declaration, proof of insurance, information about lawsuits, or even financial and corporate information.

The client will want to ensure you have the financial capability, insurance and stability to provide services and products without risk of bankruptcy or other major problems.

In some RFPs this information is mandatory and if you don't provide it exactly as required, you'll be disqualified. In others, the information is not mandatory, but may have a detrimental effect on your response. Closely review the RFP documentation to understand the mandatory submission requirements.

In some cases, you may not be able to provide information. Some private companies refuse to divulge financial information that may be required by the client. It's important to informally discuss this type of problem with the procurement representative, rather than simply say you can't provide the information in your proposal. The procurement representative can provide guidance about how to deal with the problem, and provide you with direction or issue an addendum for all bidders.

Submission and format requirements

The format of your response may be dictated by the RFP. There are many types of format requirements, but the most common include the following:

- Maximum page count.
- Minimum font size.
- Minimum margins.
- The specific format of softcopy submission, including the version of the software.
- The number of original signed copies.
- The number of other copies.
- The exact packaging and labeling requirements.

It's important that when a format is provided, you adhere to it. In some cases, this is to make it easier for the reviewers and to enforce limits that require concise responses instead of wordy sales pitches. It's easier to evaluate a shorter proposal, but it's also much harder to write one.

Whether the requirements are easy to follow or not, it's important to keep within them and find a way to make them work for you.

Example

Always follow instructions, but you can be creative:

A client required the written proposal to be provided in an Excel spreadsheet with pre-defined cells for answering specific questions.

This severely limited the bidders' ability to format the response with headings, bullet points and other techniques that make a proposal easy-to-read and information easy-to-find. Some bidders were able to introduce some formatting and other features that made their response easier to read.

Other parts of the requirements, such as the number of copies you are to provide, will relate to how the proposal will be evaluated. Carefully consider the RFP requirements and consider the process. This could be useful when considering your approach and strategy.

Process

It's important to understand the overall process used by the client in their RFP initiative. This includes site visits and bidder meetings, deadlines for submission of questions, evaluation process and criteria, presentations, negotiation, and execution of the agreement.

The overall process may include a prequalification step before the RFP is issued. This technique is used to narrow down the field so that the actual RFP evaluations include only top proponents. This is often used for large RFPs that are not only expensive and time-consuming to respond to, but also complex and resource-intensive to review and evaluate. Getting through the initial prequalification stage means you'll be competing with a smaller number of companies for the work.

Some government and corporate RFPs are open, meaning anyone can respond. Whichever approach the client takes should be part of your strategic planning. Take into consideration the type, nature and number of competitors and whether or not you know who they are.

Example

Using the process to your advantage:

For an RFP, the client posted the names of all the companies who picked up the RFP documentation.

By looking at the companies on the list, and examining their strengths and weaknesses, the bidder developed a strategy related to the competition.

Be aware that some companies pick up the RFP documentation because they want to be a subcontractor to a bidder, or to determine whether they have the minimum requirements. They may not actually bid.

Evaluation criteria and process

The evaluation of your proposal against pre-set criteria and expectations from the client will help decide whether you're selected or not. While this is always coupled with the price, the impact of your written proposal will carry weight, either to get you past the first step in the process, after which they evaluate pricing, or as part of the overall scoring. Two processes are usually used.

The first is the two-step evaluation where the technical, or written proposal, is evaluated against criteria. If you receive a minimum score, you pass the first step and your pricing is evaluated. In some cases, the technical score is not considered after you pass the first step, and the final evaluation is on pricing.

The second is an overall scoring methodology where the written proposal's evaluation score is added to the financial evaluation score for a total score. The financial score is sometimes based on a formula that gives the highest score to the lowest price, and pro-rates the other higher-priced proposals. Other formulas may be used, so you need to understand how your pricing will be evaluated to set the right strategy.

The proportion of the scoring assigned to the pricing can vary, often from 30% to 50% of the score. In a formal process, the absolute score may determine the winning bidder while other processes enable negotiations with the highest bidder if the technical written evaluation is higher than the bidder with the lowest price. It depends on the RFP rules and whether legislation governs the process. This is sometimes used when the lowest price is much lower than the other bids and it appears that the bidder may not be able to perform for the price they proposed.

Regardless of the process, the objective should be to get the highest possible score for your technical proposal. If there are any doubts or if there's a tie in pricing, you want to make the best impression on the client so they'll lean in your direction.

Negotiation

Based on the RFP process, the client may select a winner and award the contract directly, or select a preferred bidder and enter into negotiations to finalize the contract documentation and possibly elements of the services or the pricing itself.

You should know what the process is from the RFP documentation and be prepared for negotiations if they're part of the process. While you may be selected as the preferred proponent for negotiations, clients often leave their options open so that if negotiations with you fail, they can move to the next highest scoring proponent.

Some RFPs are designed to get the best proponent based on the technical submission, and pricing information is gathered primarily as data to be used in negotiating a final price.

While not common, some companies will negotiate with the two top bidders in parallel before coming to a final decision. Knowing that this is part of the process is important, and can influence your approach to the RFP.

Contract document

Sometimes a client will provide a draft contract as part of the RFP process. It is very important to understand how this is provided and what the client expects in your response. They may expect you to accept the contract terms as-is as part of your proposal submission, or they may be expecting constructive input and comments on the contract language itself. This input can be related to items you would like to see modified or clauses you would be unable to meet or agree to. Naturally, this information would end up being part of the client's evaluation process. In some cases, the client may evaluate the degree to which you'll accept their contract terms, and in others it may be a pass/fail score.

If the contract is provided in the RFP on an as-is basis with the expectation that if you win, you'll sign, be certain the contract is something you can accept. Don't assume it's something you can negotiate, since clients may move to the alternate proponent if you aren't prepared to accept the contract as-is. Be prepared to sign the contract and live up to the commitment you made in the RFP response.

Pricing

While a well-developed, persuasive proposal is a prerequisite for winning a scored RFP response, pricing is often the tipping factor. As discussed above, the RFP approach used by the client can provide you with insight on how this will factor into the final decision and how to develop your overall strategy. Whether the client will take the price as-is or negotiate with a preferred proponent is the key issue to identify.

Understanding the pricing structure and considering what level of detail the client is asking for and why will also help you with your approach. Sometimes details are requested in order to verify that you adequately priced the service delivery, and wise clients won't want to award a contract to a company who won't be able to afford to provide the necessary services.

Asking for pricing details is also a way to more appropriately compare different bidders and facilitate negotiations on pricing.

Tip | For some services that are very labor-based, asking for the proposed hours and the related labor rates enables a client to reverse engineer your pricing and make sure you're pricing the full service you're proposing.

Options

Not all RFPs ask you to provide service delivery or pricing options. If they do, this is an opportunity for you to put forward some value-added services that have true cost implications, or to propose an alternate way of either pricing or delivering the service.

Enlightened clients will ask you to provide options and innovations based on your experience and expertise with that particular product or service. Sometimes, they will specifically ask for optional pricing on services that they're not certain they want to include in the contract, or that are not quantifiable, therefore only unit pricing is needed.

If you're given the opportunity to provide options, be sure to take advantage of them. This could include options that increase services and price, or change the service levels or scope in a way that benefits the client with lower pricing while at the same time achieving the results they're looking for.

What You Need to Do to Get to the Table

Now that you've dissected the RFP, you're in a better position to understand some of the key ingredients you need to win. These ingredients become the foundation on which your entire strategy and written proposal will be based, all of which is expanded on later.

Assess needs

Strategically, this is one of the most important parts of the strategy. By understanding the needs of the client, you're better prepared to address those needs directly.

This can only be accomplished with a customized proposal response that isn't simply a cut-and-paste initiative with boilerplate material.

Assessing the client's needs includes providing a solution that addresses both the specific requirements the client has identified, and other unidentified requirements you may or should know about. This enables you to describe your solution in a way that fits with the client's stated needs and also sells your solution based on the unspoken issues that will be of interest to the client. Generic sales pitches simply won't work. You need to target the client's needs.

Develop your solution

The solution itself has to provide a benefit or solve a problem for the client. It has to address the needs of the client and make sense to them. The solution and the related benefits need to come first when developing your proposal response. It's impossible to actively write a proposal without clearly understanding how you deliver the services, how they impact the client, and what the benefits will be.

You may need to assemble a team to develop the solution for the client. Be cautious, however. While many clients seek the standardized, tried-and-tested approach of a larger organization whose core business is the service they're procuring, they also want a customized solution that addresses them as unique.

Sometimes, this doesn't match your organization's various internal departments and service group processes or approaches. If so, you need to push the issue and make sure you're developing a winning proposal, not just a cookie-cutter solution that's likely to lose.

Sometimes subtle things can be changed to make the solution customized while still retaining the essence of your efficient but standardized service delivery processes.

Gather pieces

Once the solution is established, gather the pieces you need for an effective proposal response. This includes information about the solution, terminology, position or functional titles, illustrations, diagrams, and of course the proposal text.

Past experience in providing this particular service is critical, and the client may also be asking for things such as references, organizational charts, and even resumes.

The earlier you start collecting the information the better off you'll be in the end. If you have a proposal coordinator or administrator to whom you can assign the task, they can keep track of what's requested and received to identify where pressure is required to get the material you need when you need it.

Establish your pricing model

Sometimes the proposal itself requires pricing to be provided in a very specific format with certain information broken down. If this is the case, you need to develop your pricing in accordance with the format the client has requested. Sometimes, the requirement is a total price with some of the pricing broken down into specific details.

If the client hasn't provided a specific format and structure, you should develop an approach that best suits your service.

You should consider breaking out your pricing information in more detail than you might otherwise provide. By doing this strategically, you provide information to the client about how you arrived at your total price. This may provide an incentive for them to negotiate pricing with you if they like your technical proposal but consider your total cost too high.

You should also consider providing pricing options. If there's a value-added service you're interested in providing, but it has real costs that may make your bid too expensive, include the value-added service with an incremental cost to the client as an option to your base price. That way, your base bid won't be inflated and if the client likes your optional services, they can choose to add them.

Lessons Learned

Use pricing options to deal with scope uncertainty:

A large consulting service RFP had very few details on the requirements or inputs necessary to price the work.

As a result, a bidder made assumptions for fairly high-level service and activity, with a corresponding bid price. The winning bidder was almost half the price.

A better approach would have been to bid a basic level of service with a base bid price, and include optional services along with the associated extra cost, allowing the client to decide if the extra service was worth it.

How you approach your pricing will depend on the RFP itself. If pricing is very rigid and static and scored in a certain way, you'll approach it the same way. If the scoring either does not clearly identify how price differentials are dealt with, or there's no real scoring provided, you have much more flexibility and need to take a strategic approach to providing your pricing model.

When pricing is built from the ground up, perhaps from various departments or business units within your company, make sure it's clear what your strategy is and what kind of buffer or risk premium is built in, if any. When pricing is provided at several levels, there's a danger that each level will include risk or buffer in their numbers, resulting in compounding which could price you out of the business.

Write the proposal

Beyond the technical solution and pricing, the actual written response is a key part of a successful proposal.

A sophisticated client recognizes that the technical proposal is most important to them over the duration of the contract, since successful delivery of your service will help them succeed in their own core business.

The greater the degree to which the services impact their core business, the more important it becomes. That's one of the reasons an effective and persuasive written proposal is critical to your success, all things being equal. Addressing the client needs, promoting your solution, and supporting the pricing model, is what your technical response must do well.

Playing the Game – Evaluation Scoring

If your RFP will be formally scored and evaluated, you can improve your success by fully understanding where the points are awarded and, in particular, how the price will be evaluated within the evaluation framework.

Since a successful proposal hinges on maximizing points, understanding how to get the most points will let you manage your strategy, response and pricing to ensure you get maximum points in evaluation.

When it comes to the technical portion of your proposal, key techniques to ensure you maximize your points include having the right solution that's clearly written, well-structured and strategically positioned based on scoring and evaluation. To achieve this you must hit the client's hot buttons, establish themes, mirror back to the client, and organize your information to make it easy for reviewers. All of these will be covered in detail.

You need to consider how the scoring splits between the technical elements and the price, as well as the approach the client will use to choose a winning bidder. This helps you develop your strategy.

If the technical elements are weighted higher, particularly if they're much higher than the pricing, you need to put more effort into the technical proposal. If pricing is 40 percent or more of the score, the price will be a large driver, although the written proposal will still be important if your pricing is close to one of your competitors.

Lessons Learned

Use the pricing model to your advantage:

An RFP was issued with two separate services, one with a single fixed price and the other with a percentage fee applied to actual costs.

The single, fixed-price service had a much higher proportion of the evaluation points, while the percentage fee service had a very low proportion. The bid was won by bidding the fixed price at cost and the percentage rate at a comfortable level that made up for the loss of profit on the other service.

How you manage the strategy depends on the evaluation method. If the high score bidder is awarded the bid, you need to get the high score. If there's some latitude for the client to negotiate and if you believe that they'll use this flexibility, ensure your technical proposal is very strong and position your pricing with flexibility.

In some cases, evaluation of the pricing is done by taking the lowest bid and using a formula to prorate all other bids against the lowest bid and allocated relative scores. Sometimes the spread is very narrow and sometimes it can be very large. By understanding how the scoring works and how many points are awarded to pricing as compared to the entire scoring, you can develop your strategy.

In addition, sometimes the pricing itself is split into several components depending on the service. More emphasis may be on one part of the pricing component over another. If you fully understand what the requirements are, you can manage how you price these separate components to improve your chances of winning.

Get Your Couch – You Need an Analysis

Part of the strategic planning necessary for an effective proposal response should be a modified SWOT analysis (Strengths, Weaknesses, Opportunities and Threats) that is specifically geared to your proposal response.

Rather than simply doing a standard SWOT analysis commonly done by businesses to address competitive positioning, focus the SWOT analysis on the outcomes you need to develop for a compelling proposal response. Once you've done this exercise for one proposal, you still need to revisit it to deal with the specifics of each subsequent proposal.

The outcome of a SWOT analysis should feed into your proposal response. This is the only reason you're doing it, so ensure you keep the end goal in mind throughout the process. If you start to look at things in your SWOT analysis that are outside the context of the proposal itself, you should park those issues for a future business assessment session. There will always be a temptation to use the SWOT session for more than just your proposal requirements, so be prepared to manage your time and the involvement of the participants.

Strength

Strengths should be related to the service you're proposing to client. Focus on the needs of the clients and develop clear, honest strengths that you can focus on.

A strength may also be something that's an advantage over one or more competitors, but don't focus your proposal on something that isn't strong enough to beat all of your competitors.

To assess this properly, you can't do it in isolation – you need to honestly understand who your competitors are, and where you are relative to them. Start the process by identifying all the areas that may be of interest to the client and related to the RFP.

This includes everything in the scope, relevant evaluation criteria, and other aspects of the service you're aware of that may not be identified by the client, but you believe are important.

Once you've made your list, go through each one and identify whether you have a particular strength in that area. Rather than simply saying yes or putting a checkmark next to the listing, you need to quantify the strength in a way that enables you to describe it to the client and sell it as a benefit. The strength you identify must be based on the client's position or perception. Calling something a strength and trying to promote it in the proposal when your customer simply doesn't care is a wasted effort.

Weakness

Use the same list of areas you think are of interest to the client or requirements of the RFP, and quantify each and every single item in which you're weak – either because you don't quite meet the requirements of the RFP, or because you don't have the depth of experience you believe the client is expecting. Even if you have what you think is superior experience and capability, one or more of your competitors may actually be stronger than you, and be able to demonstrate that to the client more effectively, so carefully assess your weaknesses relative to your competition.

For each of the weaknesses you've identified, quantify the weakness and identify its importance and impact on the proposal's success. Quantify how to mitigate the weakness.

Mitigation of weaknesses can be done in many ways. If you think your competition will position something that's your weakness as a strength, you can discuss the item and put doubt into the client's mind about the importance of that strength. You can also indirectly show that a competitor's perceived strength is not actually strength. This is the Ghosting technique more fully described in Part 5.

You can also find a way to turn a weakness into a strength. If the weakness was team member experience, for instance, reexamine the team members you've assigned to the project, and bring on board other team members or partners who have the necessary experience or capability. It may also require changing part of your process. You can also admit an issue or problem, and clearly describe how you've addressed it with an alternative approach meaning it's no longer a weakness.

Opportunities

Identifying the opportunities for this particular bid may provide you with information you can use to modify your approach, use a solution you may not have otherwise considered, or even provide more effective pricing.

The opportunity may include entering a new geographic market, or positioning yourself for future RFPs you may not otherwise have been considered for. If this RFP will provide you with significant new business, you may choose to organize and staff it in a different way, and to price it with entry into that new area of the marketplace as your primary goal.

If the potential new business is significant enough, this may be an opportunity for you to make changes or modifications to your product or service that will not only meet client needs, but put you in a more competitive position for future business opportunities.

Threats

Like opportunities, threats should be used to focus pricing and make decisions about the solutions and techniques you use to provide the service. This will translate into the approach you take in the proposal itself.

Threats can either be external or internal. An internal threat, for instance, may be competing priorities for resources if you win the bid. You may be pursuing other business that will stretch your ability to deliver. You need to mitigate this threat as part of your proposal response, since the client may also be aware of this.

External threats could include the success of your main competitor in recent RFPs, which makes them look like they're better than you. Your competitor may have also expanded, bought out another company, or introduced services you don't yet provide.

While all of these can be legitimate problems, identifying them honestly as threats may influence the solution or pricing you develop in response to the RFP. You can also turn around threats to your strategic benefit by identifying issues the threats could create for the client, and proactively providing a solution.

Help the Client Help Themselves

The client identified what they considered to be their requirements within the RFP documentation. Don't stop there, however. Look for issues and risks the client should be aware of, and outline how you will address these to mitigate problems. Support this by providing examples and proof of what you've done for other clients.

Clients always appreciate free advice and, in particular, service providers and suppliers who look out for their interests and help them avoid problems. During your proposal response, you gain additional credibility by accurately assessing circumstances, identifying problems or issues, and providing thoughts on how these can be mitigated or addressed, either by the clients or by you if you win.

Tip

Don't wait for them to ask:

Some RFPs will ask you to point out problems or issues you see with implementation or ongoing service delivery, and ask how you would deal with them.

Even if clients don't ask, you should tell them anyway.

If you do this well, you can clearly demonstrate your knowledge and expertise, as well as potentially put your competitor's abilities into question.

How Do You Respond to a Bad RFP?

The simple answer is to take advantage of the situation. If the RFP is poorly written and structured, you have an opportunity to put information forward that you feel is relevant.

Very few good questions

Frequently, questions asked by the client in RFPs are not well thought out, and won't make it easy for the client to determine the best bidder. In this case, be sure to answer the question that's asked, but also take the opportunity to expand with related information you feel will put your proposal ahead of the rest.

If you can add new sections or expand on the questions you're expected to respond to, simply add the information where it makes sense. If you feel you can't stray from the RFP at all, look closely at all the sections or questions, and add the information you need in sub-sections or sub-questions to the existing structure. Just be sure to clearly address the original information the client requested.

When you do this, provide the information under headings that are stated as questions. This will be more effective than simply adding additional information at the end of the original question.

Questions that are too broad

Some questions, such as "explain your approach," are so broad that it's difficult to understand exactly what the client is interested in. In this case, refer back to the evaluation criteria and use the question as a basis for structuring the answer to that specific question.

You could even use the evaluation criteria items as headings within your response to the broad question. This is an easy way to ensure the information you provide matches up well with the criteria being evaluated.

Of course, based on your strategy, you should have other key items that you want to get across to the client. Base these items on themes, hot buttons or other issues and considerations you know are important and will give you a higher score. These key items should also be prominently identified within the response.

While at first a broad question may appear to be difficult to respond to, it's actually something you can shape and influence to deliver your message more effectively.

A single question with multiple parts

The client may ask a single question that actually has multiple parts. Separately identify each of the question's parts as a heading, and respond to each individually and directly. This way, the evaluators will be able to clearly see the information you provide, and relate it directly to the part of the question you're answering. It also makes sure you don't miss any part of the question.

When structuring your response using the same format as the RFP response requirements, you can include the separate questions as sub-questions under the main one.

If you reword any of the questions or sub-questions to make headings, make sure you still retain the original question text. Otherwise, you may miss a key part of the question.

Repetitive questions

Sometimes, especially if the RFP questions have been developed by several groups within the client, or by committee, you'll find questions that are very similar if not identical in different places throughout the RFP. For instance, the RFP may ask about quality assurance related to three different aspects of service delivery. Since quality assurance, as an example, is usually a service-wide initiative, you have an opportunity to repeat some of the fundamental elements about your quality assurance program while at the same time adding elements that are very specific to that part of the service. Resist the temptation to simply refer the client to the previous question.

Example

Don't make this mistake for repetitive questions:

In a poorly-structured RFP, the client asked the exact same set of questions in each of the nine services within the scope.

While some of the questions could be answered specifically for each service, the answer to several questions was the same for all services. Some respondents made the mistake of answering the question once and then simply answering 'See Above' for each subsequent response.

The best way to deal with this is not by simply repeating verbatim what you said earlier. Acknowledge that the question is essentially the same and that how you provide the services is consistent with the previous answer. Then repeat the key elements of the answer, particularly the ones that are key to getting higher evaluation scores, and add new information that focuses on that specific scope area. For instance, summarize the previous answer and add a heading that allows you to say something specific about the scope area.

It's possible that different people will evaluate different sections. If this is likely, you should repeat the full answer, not just summarize. If any parts of the answer are unique to the specific question, section or scope, clearly identify the unique parts and separate them from the common areas so if it's the same evaluator, they won't skip over it and miss the key part of the answer. Don't forget that if there are different evaluators for different sections, their issues and interests will be different so you need to speak to the evaluators individually.

Confusing or ambiguous information

If the instructions or information provided to you in the RFP are ambiguous or confusing, it's in your best interests to clarify with the client. Instead of doing this through the formal Q&A process, bring it, if you can, to their attention informally through a phone call or email to prevent potential embarrassment if they've missed something important.

The worst thing you can do is speculate about the client's intentions. When in doubt, clarify.

Not asking for experience

Some proposals will simply ask you how you plan on providing the service based on the scope and information provided in the RFP. If they have not clearly asked you to provide your experience, take the opportunity at the end of the each section or question to include a heading and demonstrate the experience you have.

This approach can be used for any other information you think is relevant, and it must specifically be identified to the client for their evaluation. Even if it isn't specifically listed evaluation criteria, explaining your capabilities with examples will positively influence results.

Not enough information provided

Not all RFPs have detailed scope requirements. This makes it a challenge to respond with a technical solution and price that is likely to match client expectations. Sometimes, the client does this on purpose if they're unclear about the requirements and are looking for creative solutions. In other cases, the client may not understand what's required to develop and deliver an effectively-targeted, well-priced proposal.

In some cases, you may want to ask the client for more information, however it's possible that if they haven't provided the information as part of the RFP process already, they don't have it.

When you don't have all the information you need, the best option is to do your research and develop a bid you think will most likely meet their requirements. You can hedge your bets by providing assumptions or alternatives if you're concerned about missing the mark and having a competitor offer a lesser service at a lower price. This is particularly effective for services where there may be a wide range of service levels or approaches with very different cost structures. Another way of achieving this is by providing the lowest base price you can with options that can be added at an additional cost.

They ask for something you don't want to provide

If the client asks for information you can't or don't want to provide for corporate or confidentiality reasons, be it a mandatory requirement or not, you need to address that directly with the client before you submit your proposal.

An example of this is detailed financial information. Clients may request this information to verify you have the financial resources and stability to provide services. Some private companies won't provide this information due to confidentiality, and some public companies may not be able to provide it to the level of detail that's required.

If confidentiality is the issue, you may be able to address this with the client by providing them with a different method for gaining the financial confidence they need in your organization. This may mean restricted access to the information by a key individual within the client's organization, or through the client bank for instance. If level of detail is a problem, you can address this with the client to see what would be acceptable. In any case, dealing directly with the client to resolve this issue before submitting your bid is the best approach.

Another request, especially with large-service RFPs, is asking about your market strategy. The intent is to understand your company better and determine whether the business you're bidding on is truly part of your core strength and direction.

You may not want to provide this kind of information in a bid document. You may, however, be willing to discuss this verbally as part of a presentation. Ask the client whether your solution is acceptable. If it isn't acceptable, evaluate whether answering this question will truly compromise your organization, and whether or not answering the question will jeopardize your ability to win the bid. This approach can be used for anything you feel you cannot answer for confidentiality or competitive reasons as part of the formal RFP process.

Go Bold or Go Home

If you're submitting a proposal to a client, your intent should be to win it. You and your company need to apply the appropriate effort to the proposal, usually related to the importance and size of the potential contract.

That doesn't mean you shouldn't use the same techniques and principals on smaller and less important proposals. You simply scale back the level of effort.

In order to win, be bold in your approach, and ensure you have the resources and information you need to convince the client you're the best.

There's only one situation where you wouldn't write a proposal to win. For various reasons, including reputation or future opportunity, you may feel compelled to submit a proposal even if you don't think you have a good chance of winning or you aren't interested in the business. It's still important to put forward a proposal that reflects your company's capabilities, image and professionalism. Don't be tempted to submit a poorly written proposal.

Cafeteria Pricing

When you have the flexibility, providing alternate or optional pricing in your proposal will increase the chances of the client finding a match between your proposal and your pricing, and select you as the winning bidder.

This includes providing your core base pricing in addition to options either with reduced or increased service levels or other features. It can include other services the client hasn't specifically asked for.

Lessons Learned

Propose optional specifications or scope:

Sometimes the specifications provided by the client have been used for a while, yet changes in the industry, shifting priorities, or your experience can result in different specifications that achieve the same results with lower cost.

Provide the pricing based on the client specifications, and then provide optional pricing based on your revised specifications.

You can also include value-added services that you don't want to include in the pricing in case you price yourself out of the competition. The best way to deal with this is to include them as an optional service as part of your proposal. Position them as a separate price that would be added to the base price, or provide two prices – the base price and another one that includes the new value-added service. This works for services the client may not have asked for. If you deliver them as a bundled service, the client will get a more attractive price.

Example

Appeal to their interests with an optional price:

In a bid where the pricing was largely based on the staffing level, the base proposal included the types of resources required to meet the scope.

An alternative was provided with two additional resources in an area that was known to be a problem for the client and would integrate well into the base services.

From a pure marketing and sales perspective, there's a reason why many things you buy have different 'levels' sold at various price points. This includes sodas or fries at fast food outlets sold in small, medium and large sizes, and manufacturers with different brands targeted at budget, regular and premium levels.

If you have an opportunity, particularly in a sole source or unsolicited bid, provide pricing options to the customer. Target your middle option as the one you think is most likely, and then provide a pared-down option and a higher-level option.

Tip

In *Yes!: 50 Scientifically Proven Ways to Be Persuasive*, the authors describe how adding a third premium option increases sales of the next lower option. This is the same principle of offering small, regular and large size soda or popcorn.

Providing alternatives in your pricing, particularly a lower alternative, is very useful when the client is requesting something in their specification contract or proposal requirements that is more than they need, or causes unnecessary costs.

Example

Recommend changes that reduce costs:

Response times for service delivery that are the same in urban centers and remote rural locations may not be reasonable.

To meet the requirements in the rural locations, the costs will be higher, yet the need for the same response time may not exist or the standard in the area for similar services may be a longer response time. If the response time doesn't seem to match the nature of the requirements, the sensitivity, or the urgency, recommend a change in the service level and a related reduction in the pricing.

This approach enables you to provide that service at a lower cost with a more reasonable level of service, and will increase your credibility to the client by identifying this and providing them with an option. The client may look differently at other bidders who would have either included a higher price for the unreasonable service level, or ignored the extra costs with the assumption they can manage expectations.

When you include optional pricing, be sure to clearly document the changes and ensure you're coordinating the pricing with the text. Go back and look at your written material and ensure it's properly described. By identifying areas where savings can be realized with a minimal or zero impact on actual service, the client will look at your proposal in a more favorable light. You will also demonstrate your knowledge in reducing cost, and therefore revenue, so your credibility will go up.

Surviving Bad Situations

While it would be nice to be in a position of advantage when you write your proposal, it's not always the case. Sometimes, you have some hurdles to cross. Not all are obvious, but all of them can be easily dealt with if approached strategically.

You are the incumbent

Being the incumbent can be a disadvantage. The unfortunate reality is that even if the client is satisfied with what you're doing, they may feel other providers have something else to offer. The risk to you depends partly on the difficultly of transition to another contractor.

Your competition may be very interested in taking the work away from you, and do everything they can to win the business. They may have been talking to the client, since they would know when the contract was coming up for re-bid, and they may have a better understanding than you realize. If you haven't been discussing renewal and/or re-bid with the client, you're behind your competition, even if you're already providing services to the client.

When it comes to pricing, you have a much better handle on the true costs of servicing the client than your competitors, but that assumes the scope and requirements won't change. It also puts you at a disadvantage. Since you understand the costs, you'll probably have the most realistic pricing – which may be higher than your competitor since you'll account for things they don't know.

Since the competitors don't know the realities of providing service to the client, your competition may either over-price or under-price. If you understand the marketplace and how attractive the client is to your competition, or how hungry they may be for new business, you can factor this into your strategy.

This is the same issue you have when you bid on work about which you don't have details. The nature of the RFP evaluation, and how pricing is handled, will dictate whether this is or is not an advantage.

An important factor in pricing is transition costs. As the incumbent, there shouldn't be any transition costs unless the scope and requirements have changed significantly, or you're proposing changes that are expensive to implement, such as a new IT system. Your competition will have transition costs that will inflate their pricing. The impact and visibility will depend on how the RFP pricing submission is structured. Some RFPs for large service contracts include a line item for transition costs. Some companies won't include any transition cost in the detailed pricing, and either eat the costs, or build the costs into their overall price. It's important to highlight the savings that the client would have by staying with you. Clients often underestimate the costs and efforts required for a transition, both in the service price and in their own organization.

Even if the client appears to be completely satisfied with your services, you may still be at risk. If you've been providing services for a while, they may feel that there are better alternatives, and be willing to switch to get different service.

Whether they're satisfied or not, the client may feel they can get better quality service, or lower pricing, with another provider, and be willing to switch to find out, particularly if your competition tells a better story than you do.

Rather than assuming you have the incumbent-advantage, you need to work just as hard on the proposal as you would to win new business.

Tip

Sometimes you know too much. This means you won't make assumptions or take risks that your competition, who really want the client's business, will take.

You need to sell to them as if they're a new client.

You may be tempted to propose changes for the new contract to entice the client. This may include new processes or technology that you're actually using with new clients, but haven't rolled out to current clients. Approach this very carefully. The client may wonder why you're holding out on them and offering it now just because they're re-bidding the business.

You should start making these changes before the end of the contract, or at least start discussing with the client and explain why you haven't implemented them under the current contract, whether due to uncertainty about recovering implementation costs over the remaining term, compatibility with the financial or organizational structure, or just that it doesn't match the client's current systems or approach.

Of course, making some changes early to show goodwill to the client and give them a taste of what you can provide is a good strategy. But be careful not to make changes too close to the RFP release, or it may appear to be only to influence the bid.

As the incumbent, you also need to illustrate the disadvantages and risks of switching, and demonstrate clearly that switching is not the right thing to do. Don't overestimate how much the impact of a transition will influence the client to retain you. Their longer-term considerations will always override the short-term effort of a transition.

You may feel you know how the client feels about your services, but you shouldn't be too complacent. If your information comes from field or operational staff, take the time to meet with the client at mid- and senior-levels, both in operations and their procurement/contracting group. Ask probing, difficult questions that will give you a true picture and the information you need for an effective proposal. Do this research well before the end of your contract – it should be an effective part of the client management and retention strategy, and a key part of your RFP response strategy.

What you learn will either surprise you or confirm what you already know. Either way, this information will help you gain back the advantage.

Your competitor is the incumbent

It's traditionally a disadvantage if you aren't the incumbent however, as described above, that isn't always the case. It also depends on the reason the client has issued the RPF.

The client will either be:

- **Neutral** – not wanting to change, but not strongly tied to the incumbent, they may have been required to issue an RFP.
- **Changing** – they have reasons to try a different service company.
- **Not Changing** – They don't have a specific reason to switch suppliers, and the RFP process is simply an exercise because they were required to issue an RFP.

Your chances of winning business from the incumbent will depend partly on which of the three reasons are motivating the client. Sometimes you can see evidence of the client's intentions in the RFP process, documentation and requirements.

If you aren't the incumbent, consider the issues identified above for the incumbent, and that the incumbent often has their own hurdles to overcome and there may not be clear benefits for them. These issues mirror your situation and some of the disadvantages to the incumbent may be advantages for you.

A key disadvantage is that client doesn't know your organization or your capabilities. If you knew the RFP was going to be issued, you should have already been preparing, doing research, increasing your exposure to the client, and even meeting with them in advance of their RFP development. You could even provide the client with information about issues or items to include in their requirements, or questions that may not otherwise have considered. The intent is that they will provide you with some kind of advantage.

In the RFP response, you need to clearly demonstrate why you're different and can provide better service than the incumbent. If you can find out what the client likes or dislikes about their current service provider, you can use this information in the proposal response.

Changing service providers can introduce risks both to the client's core business and internally. While this won't always stop the client from switching, you want to make it as painless as possible. Focusing attention on the transition provides confidence that if the client switches to you, you can minimize the risk and the workload during the transition.

New entry to the marketplace

If you're entering a new marketplace, whether it's a client segment, service, or geographic area in which you don't have a presence, you'll be at a big disadvantage.

The client may not want to take a risk on you, since service failure will impact their business and reputation. The client will have doubts as to whether you're truly capable of providing the service they need.

You need to illustrate other cases where you've been a new entrant and have succeeded, or lay out a clear plan as to how you'll ramp up to provide services with little risk to the client. This must be backed up with evidence and testimonials.

Surviving this situation also includes tapping into the resources you have in your organization. Find someone who has the experience needed, and ensure they're identified as a prominent individual within the service delivery team, or are deeply involved in the transition phase and in helping develop the operational model going forward.

Example

Dig deep to find your advantage:

A company was bidding on delivering their service to a business segment they didn't currently serve.

When exploring how to deal with this disadvantage, we found an existing employee who used to deliver the services for the specific client many years ago.

This employee was added to the proposal as a transition lead along with a write-up describing the advantage of having her on the team because of her specific experience with the service and the client.

You should also identify any related activities or services that fit within the new market you're entering.

Finding characteristics that are common in other business that you do for other clients, and matching them up with existing clients or potential clients to demonstrate you have the ability to meet their needs and understand them, is one of the ways you can mitigate this particular issue.

Tip

If you're trying to provide services to a company with unique characteristics, your experience in other markets with similar characteristics can help bridge the experience gap.

Digging deep for resources with past experience with the client or the market, and then putting those resources front and center in your proposal will also help mitigate concerns about not knowing their requirements.

If other bidders are the new entrants to the marketplace, you need to both promote the importance of your current experience in the market, and underscore the risks to the client if they bring in an inexperienced provider. Use the ghosting techniques identified in Part 5 to illustrate the risks involved if they chose the new entry over you. Remember, if you're the new entrant to the market, your competition may use the same techniques on you.

Summary

Strategy means fully understanding what you need to win, and positioning yourself as the best choice. Do this by understanding what the needs, hot buttons, issues and criteria are, and addressing them directly. Assess your organization against your competition, and use that information to position yourself as the only choice. Take advantage of bad RFPs, and eliminate perceptions and questions before they're raised.

Techniques You Can Use:

- ✓ Do a SWOT analysis to understand the issues you need to address.
- ✓ Conduct a strategy session and decide how to win.
- ✓ Understand the evaluation criteria and position yourself.
- ✓ Structure your pricing to get you to the table.

Traps To Avoid:

- ✖ Don't miss the opportunity to take advantage of a bad RFP.
- ✖ Don't let perceptions sabotage your efforts.
- ✖ Don't assume you have the advantage if you're the incumbent.

Your Action Plan to Write Better Proposals:

Based on this chapter, list several things you need to do or must do differently to win more business with your proposals.

Priority	Things to Do

Part 4
Figuring Out What the Client Really Wants

By putting yourself in the client's shoes, you'll write a better proposal. But it's not as easy as it looks. Getting all the information and assessing what's true and what's not is the first step. You must then link that with the services and solutions you provide to make the offer compelling to the client.

The following techniques are included in this section:

- Start working before the RFP is issued.
- Do your research and incorporate what you learn.
- Figure out what really matters to the client, not just what they say matters.
- Give the client what they want.

> *"I never found a client's business problem that could be solved solely through advertising."*
>
> *– Lee Clow, Chairman TBWA\Worldwide*

Do You Know What the Client Wants?

Understanding their intent

When responding to an RFP, understanding the client and what they really want is sometimes harder than it seems. Whether you have face-to-face discussions or are relying on the RFP documentation, you still may not understand what the client really wants.

While sometimes this ambiguity may be intentional to test bidders or favor an incumbent, often it's not and is merely a result of internal issues, lack of clarity in communication, or because, internally, the client has multiple views about what's needed.

Example

Understanding what the client wants can make a difference:

For an RFP that included various geographical areas and several separate services, the RFP indicated that bidders didn't necessarily have to bid on all areas or all services.

One service provider couldn't service all areas so chose not to bid. Another couldn't provide all the separate services so they only bid on the ones that were their core strength.

The client ended up awarding all geographic areas and all services to one of the few companies that bid on everything.

The first company understood the client's goals, regardless of what they said in the RFP. The second company didn't, and wasted time and effort bidding on something they couldn't have won because there were competitors who knew what the client really wanted, which was to deal with only one provider.

Don't take information at face value. Dig deeper to clearly understand what the real intent is based on your understanding of the market, the client and the circumstances of the RFP. If you let your preconceived notions guide you, you'll end up wasting your time.

Reading between the lines

It would be nice to read proposal documents and completely understand what the client wants. Unfortunately, that's rarely the case. There are times when the client can't or doesn't want to say what they really want. That's why it's important to understand the client and do research before the RFP is actually issued. If you only have the RFP, read it carefully and, rather than taking what's said literally, read between the lines and understand why the client has said what they did, or why they're asking specific questions.

> **Tip** Seemingly innocent questions, such as asking for the percentage of your total business the client's new business would represent, may have underlying reasons.
>
> The client may want to know whether they'll be a large, important client to you, or a small one who may not receive much attention. The client may also want to ensure you aren't taking on business volume you can't manage.
>
> By understanding the reasons behind the questions, you can position yourself more favorably with the client.

When possible, discuss requirements with the client before the RFP is issued, and carefully assess what they say compared to what ends up in the RFP. Find other individuals familiar with the service or the client and get their input. Try to reconcile inconsistent information and be careful of opinions that may not be current or relevant. While this is not an easy process, determining the client's real intent, rather than what they put in print, may provide strategic approaches to the RFP response that will help you win the business.

Use your research on the client to help formulate and understand what's behind what they're asking for. If there's an incumbent and they've gone out to bid even though they had an opportunity to renew with the incumbent, that should tell you something. By understanding more about the reasons, you'll be more successful in your bid response.

The bid documentation may say that price is not the deciding factor, and that other issues or characteristics of the service are more important. This may even be reflected in the evaluation criteria. However, by reading the documentation carefully and understanding the process and the client, you can validate the client's probable approach to evaluation.

To learn more about the influence of pricing, look at the client's history and research the client to understand how they represent themselves to their own customers, what their position is in the marketplace, how they deal with suppliers, and how well they're doing financially.

Lessons Learned

Be aware of all that factors that impact the Client's needs:

Before an RFP was formally released, the client indicated they were not looking for low pricing and that improved service quality was the priority.

By the time the RFP process got underway, the downturn in the economy had completely changed the client's outlook and the dynamics of the evaluation, yet the change in approach wasn't clearly stated – you had to read between the lines.

If price seems to be the prevailing concern, you can take a more creative approach to responding. The client may welcome a proposed scope or service-level reduction along with a price reduction if it's open and transparent with minimal impact on the client's core business. While the bid documentation will always talk about the service the client needs you to provide, the service almost always has a direct and sometimes important impact on the client's own customers, even if this is not explicitly identified in the bid package. By reading between the lines and understanding this linkage, you're in a better position to respond to the RFP and clearly demonstrate that you understand how important the service is to the client's core business and their own customers, and how you will ensure the client is successful, even with a low price.

Reading between the lines means involving more than just yourself in the assessment. Others within your company who have dealt with the client and external contacts with direct experience with the client may be able to shed some light on what the client is asking for beyond what they've put in the documentation. Don't overlook these other resources for this very important part of the process.

Hot buttons

While hot buttons are covered in more detail in Part 3, the client's hot buttons are something else you need to establish, whether they're stated or not.

Hot buttons may be things with a direct impact on the client, or things the client is trying to avoid based on their past experience. These may be clear in the RFP documentation, but more often than not, your understanding of the client and their environment will help you to identify the hot buttons. As a result you'll be in a better position to address these critical items in your proposal.

Issues

When trying to understand what the client needs, it helps to understand the issues the client is currently facing that impact the service you're proposing, and to address these issues as part of your strategic process.

The issues themselves may be specific to the client, or generally applicable to the service or the client's industry. They may be based on circumstances, such as whether or not you're the incumbent, the issue of transition, or perhaps the impact of the change in specifications, service levels or other elements of the service itself.

Issues can be industry-wide. For example, when corporate accountability legislation came into effect, many corporate entities also required compliance from their own suppliers.

Environmental issues, energy conservation, employee and union issues, on-time delivery, political sensitivities and other factors can be issues you need to address effectively. You gain the advantage by clearly demonstrating how you'll mitigate or solve the issues for the client.

Even if the issues are not specifically rated or scored in the evaluation, demonstrating your understanding and knowledge, and providing solutions, will have a positive impact when the client is evaluating other elements, particularly if they also impact or touch upon those elements.

As mentioned previously, your ability to identify issues that clients don't realize exist, and then proposing solutions, may impress the client and improve your chances of success. Just don't go too far – you need to keep the tone positive.

Features, benefits and unique selling points that matter

These are all things that help you sell. By understanding the client's needs and how they relate to what you have to offer, you can talk about them in a way that matches up your service offerings with the client. By doing this directly, the client clearly sees the link between what you're offering and what they require.

Example

This text doesn't focus on the message or explain a competitive advantage – it just gives the facts:

"The majority of our call centre activities are done by in-house staff. Our main Client Support Centre is located in Yorkton and has over 100 full-time employees. Additional centres are located across Canada, servicing your needs. We also have a small 12-employee back-up centre at our Guelph head office. All of our call centres offer bilingual service and are accessible via a dedicated toll free number or by email."

To identify your benefits effectively, you first need a clear understanding of the client's needs. The next step is to list all the features and benefits along with your unique selling points, and to match those with the client requirements. After you've matched them, you can decide how to address the needs within the proposal, and link directly to the client needs. Where possible, ensure that your benefits link directly to the scoring matrix and evaluation criteria.

When you establish your benefits and unique selling points, you have to fully understand your competition's position and their benefits or unique selling points to be certain yours are in fact unique. The client will be reading similar material from your competition and if you overstate your capabilities and benefits, you could lose credibility.

Example

Don't oversell your benefits:

A service provider who felt they had a clear advantage over their competition based on their way of doing business overestimated the impact.

The service provider appeared arrogant and actually highlighted a weakness the client was concerned about.

Do They Really Care About Value-Added?

Value-added is a buzzword you may see being requested in RFPs and if not, you're likely trying to figure out how to provide it in your proposals. The simple question is what 'value added' really means and whether it will have material impact on your proposal.

When it comes right down to it, so-called value-added in a proposal should really be your competitive advantage. However, if it looks like it's important to the client that you provide 'value-added', or the value-added is part of the evaluation criteria or scoring, you need to find things that the client will consider value-added.

This sometimes ends up being a pricing issue – what you want to provide as value-added services, and how much they impact the price.

Unless it's explicitly identified how value-added services or features will influence the client to select you as the winner, assume that any value-added items you provide will simply give you the edge in the existing evaluation model.

Your main goal is to clearly demonstrate your capabilities and the fact that you're the best choice to provide the requirements identified in the RFP.

Value-added can be the icing on the cake. However, you do need to consider the costs and impacts value-added may have on your final proposal price, and the impact on evaluation scoring. Start by focusing on 'value-added' that is simply part of how you operate your business efficiently.

If you can provide value-added without having a negative impact on your proposal price, either through technology, volume or efficiency, simply identify the value these items provide, and explain the results for the client.

Don't make the mistake of pulling things out of your normal service and calling them value-added unless they're clearly value-added items. This will be apparent to the client and cause you to lose credibility.

Value-added doesn't always need to be incorporated within your base price. One way to structure a proposal with significant value-added items is to provide an optional service with optional pricing.

Some RFPs will ask for options while others will not. Regardless of whether the clients ask or not, if you have some attractive options, you should propose them. Make it clear that they're separate and distinct from your main proposal. Be sure to read the submission requirements carefully to ensure this approach won't disqualify you.

Example

Positioning 'value-add' without pricing yourself out of the competition:

An RFP specifically required adhering to current practices, which were very manual and not assisted by a computerized system.

The pricing structure was for management and administration only, with the direct costs of labor as a flow-through to the client.

This meant a computerized system would have added costs to the price, but the direct cost savings were not considered in the evaluation.

Adding the computerized system would have been value-added, but the higher price would have lost the bid.

The bid was submitted with the base requirements, however the capability and experience of implementing and using a computerized system to drive efficiencies and reduce direct costs was clearly identified as a benefit to the client.

After the bid was won, the client requested implementation of a computerized system at the client's cost. This strategy helped win the bid.

This is an example of why strategy around the entire process, both the technical solution and the pricing, is so critical.

Can You Give Them What They Need?

Understanding what the client needs will help you win their business. Specific requirements will either be clearly identified in the RFP, or your research and strategic planning will have identified the specific requirements you must provide to win the business. These requirements can be addressed specifically in your service solution or technical proposal.

There are other more general considerations you should include in your proposal strategy for the client. They apply to almost all clients, whether they're clearly identified in the RFP or not. It's worth examining the fundamentals so you can build these into your proposal response. Consider other things the client may need that haven't been identified, and figure out how to incorporate them.

Consistency

Consistent service is always appreciated, particularly when the services are delivered over time, or a large geographical area. The client usually wants the service to be delivered in the same way with the same quality everywhere. While this may seem easy to do, it isn't always the case. Being able to provide evidence of how you maintain consistency will give you an advantage, all else being equal.

Tip | Consistency usually goes along with quality processes, so this should be one of the benefits of your Quality Management process.

Consistency isn't just in service delivery, it's also in the client/supplier interface and relationship, including reporting and communications.

If you have a way of demonstrating that you currently provide a consistent service that meets service requirements, your proposal will be that much stronger.

Dependability

Dependability is critical to all clients, particularly when your service directly impacts the client's core business and the services they provide to internal or external customers.

If the client can depend on you to deliver, they're in a better position to serve their own clients. For this, you need to demonstrate your track record and how you ensure dependability. Examples of dependable behavior or successes with other clients, as well as measurements, should be used to provide the evidence. Sometimes the client will ask for this specifically and if they don't, be sure to tell them.

Tip | Tell stories or provide examples of how you provided dependable service to clients, such as during natural disasters, extreme weather, strikes, or other extenuating situations.

Confidence

If the client doesn't have confidence in your organization and the people you put forward to work on their account, nothing else will matter.

You gain the client's confidence through your company's reputation, clear evidence in your proposal, and even in your formal presentation or other interactions with the client during the process.

Gaining confidence from the client requires a solid track record, whether as a company, or the resources you propose as part of the RFP. If there are issues about your past performance which cast doubt, you need to mitigate these concerns by raising them yourself, and identifying how you have changed your process, improved quality or even brought in new experienced staff with the right expertise.

Understanding how the client perceives your organization is important to deciding how to address confidence in your RFP response. In any case, lack of confidence by the client will have a negative impact on everything else you say in the proposal, and will likely result in a lower evaluation in many areas.

Example | **Past performance gives your client confidence:**

Clients often ask for examples of current business that match their needs. They do this to gain confidence that you can do the work and have sufficient experience. When providing the examples, don't just describe the work you do, clearly match it up with the client's requirements to instill confidence.

Low maintenance

No client wants a service provider who will be hard to deal with or take lots of effort to manage. Even if it's an important service, the client always has other more important issues to deal with.

Convincing the client that you take an active approach – so they don't have to – will help your proposal. Outline your management process, including how you convey information, and how you deal with issues. Keep the client informed, and the steps you take to minimize their efforts will be welcome.

Example | **Try not to burden your client:**

If you're not already the incumbent, outline your transition plan with emphasis on the minimum level of effort required from the client for a successful transition. Not only will that show you value the client's time, you'll also show them that transitioning from their incumbent to you is an easy option.

Espionage, the Modern (and Legal) Way

Even before you start preparing your response, you need to learn as much as you can about the client and your competition.

You can gather a considerable amount of useful information from the Internet without a lot of effort, and can use this information to help develop your strategy, or show clients you have a solid understanding of their issues and what they need.

Use the information within your response to help describe how you can solve the client's issues or support them. This is most effective when you can repeat back to the client certain terminology, phrases or other nuances you have picked up in your research. Use what you know about the competition to give your proposal more leverage, but don't name the competition specifically or be negative about them.

Example

Small details can improve your proposal:

Simple research on the client's website found key terms and processes that were incorporated into the proposal response and process flow diagrams.

It also uncovered an organization chart that identified how the service fit into the organization, and who was responsible for the service. A Google search revealed their previous jobs and what they were involved in. The proposal emphasized experiences that matched with their background and interests. This fostered familiarity and may have influenced how the proposal was scored. Every little bit counts.

Look for the latest annual reports and review them for information you can use. Search for news articles and press releases about the client and competition, including what's on their own web sites. For government and other public organizations, search for committee agendas or meeting minutes.

If you have the names of key client representatives, search for them on the Internet and learn from any associations they belong to, articles by or about them, presentations they have done, or other information that can indicate their interests and issues they've dealt with and care about.

Speak with existing client employees and contacts before the RFP is issued to beat the moratorium on contact with the client or client's employees during the RFP process. Even if the process isn't very formal or rigid, be careful when engaging the client during the process. If you're working on a sole source or unsolicited proposal, you will need to talk to people within the organization to get sufficient information.

Seek out past employees from the client and your competition and interview them to get insights, including issues, perceptions and preferences, terminology and problems you may not otherwise have known about. Use this information carefully, since it is very subjective. These individuals may not be plugged in at the right levels, and some information may not reflect the current situation. Even if you're responding to a smaller proposal, a short networking discussion over coffee could provide information you can use.

Talk to your own employees. You may be surprised to find out what past connections they have with your competitors or the client. It's useful to bring them in when you're developing your strategy. They may not be able to contribute a lot to the proposal writing itself, but they can certainly provide a great deal of insight on how you develop your proposal.

Care and Feeding of Evaluators

In most cases, winning a proposal means convincing the evaluators that you deserve the highest score. While your proposal has to be good enough in the first place, you can improve your chances for a higher score when you consider the effort required by the evaluators, and make it easier for them.

The first step is to carefully review the evaluation process and method. In most cases, a scoring matrix will be provided, indicating how many points are being assigned to various parts of your proposal. The second part, which is not always initially obvious, is the criteria the evaluators use to evaluate. If you look at this as a checklist the evaluators will use to make sure you've properly covered all parts of the evaluation criteria, you can then structure your response accordingly to make it easy for the evaluators.

In addition, you should focus on the key words and headings the RFP uses, and make sure you've used the same ones in your response. This enables the evaluators to link what you're saying with their evaluation criteria. This method will enable the evaluators to see the evidence that you put forward as a basis for each of the criteria.

Don't be afraid to repeat some information if necessary to ensure your response lines up with the evaluation criteria. You're simply reinforcing the information you provide.

If the RFP has not provided you with explicit evaluation criteria, you should try to establish what the criteria might be, and be consistent in how you present it so the evaluators will see the information consistently.

In addition to focusing on the evaluation criteria when you respond to the RFP, you should ask yourself the following questions as you're developing your response:

- ☑ Have you made it easy to evaluate?
- ☑ Have you made your solution clear and easy to understand?
- ☑ Have you demonstrated your capability?
- ☑ Have you structured your proposal logically or in accordance with the requirements?
- ☑ Have you addressed all the evaluation elements?
- ☑ Have you answered all the questions?
- ☑ Have you oversold with fluff?

- ☑ Have you been too arrogant?
- ☑ Have you provided concrete information, or theories and generalities?
- ☑ Have you made it simple?
- ☑ Have you pointed the evaluators to the places you want them to read?

Don't Let Perception Overwhelm Reality

Perception can be a problem in two ways. First, your perception of the client and their requirements may not be true, and could taint your proposal response. Second, the client's perception of your organization and your service may not be valid, and will influence how they evaluate your proposal.

Tip | In *The 22 Immutable Laws of Marketing* by Al Ries and Jack Trout, the 4th law of marketing is the law of perception. The authors state that marketing is not a battle of products, it's a battle of perceptions.

Your perception of the client

It's very important to base your proposal response strategy on fact and information, not your perceptions, since perceptions are often incorrect. One of the easiest ways to alienate the reviewers is to frame your message around something you perceive is true when it isn't. Since the client is doing the evaluation, they have the facts and the data, and they understand the reality surrounding their circumstance. If you don't make an effort to abandon your preconceived notions and establish the facts, you may miss the mark or even offend the client.

Make sure that information you use as a basis for your response, or when developing your strategy, isn't rumor or somebody's perception of the client. Do more research and challenge opinions until you're convinced you have facts and a solid understanding.

Even information you get from the client's past employees should be verified and carefully considered. The information will always be filtered through personal experiences, and even their position within the client organization. The information may also be old and not reflect the client now.

Their perception of you

The client's perception of your organization and capabilities can easily influence their evaluation of your proposal, even when there's a rigid evaluation matrix and criteria. It's simply human nature.

Because of the impact of perception, it's important to understand the rumors, innuendo or other perceptions that are in the marketplace related to your organization or services. When possible, understand the specific perceptions the client holds.

This includes the perception of senior members of the client organization, the individuals performing the evaluation, and any consultants or transaction advisors, including technical experts, involved in the process. This is especially important if the client does not have experience working with you.

The client may have perceptions you need to counteract. Consultants may share their own perceptions with the client and they will be factored into the advice they give the client about evaluation and even negotiations down the road.

Example

Consider how things look to the client.

If you weren't renewed with a client recently and lost their business, there will be rumors about why you lost the business, most likely negative. This will have an impact on evaluators.

Through your network and through discussions with other people in the industry, you need to get an honest idea of how you're perceived in the industry. If you've worked on proposals for this client, you should have gained some information as a result of either successful or unsuccessful bids, and have a solid understanding of what their perception may be. As discussed earlier, this is another reason why debriefings are very important and can provide you with additional information you need to improve your bids going forward.

Also, if there are key procurement or outsourcing consultants who work on major RFP projects, introduce your company to them and seek input and feedback between proposals. It's in their interests to understand the marketplace and clear up any perceptions so that they can provide the best service to their clients.

If you know there's a large RFP coming out, contact the client and have discussions in advance. Ask direct and probing questions to get the client's impressions before the RFP is issued and your communications are limited.

Whenever you hear about a negative perception, you need to deal with it directly as if it were real. Don't discount it because you know it isn't true. As long as others believe it, it will have the same effect as if it were true.

Either clear up the perceptions before the RFP is issued, or deal with it through facts and information in your proposal. Don't be afraid to identify the perception and then demonstrate why it isn't true. Leaving any doubt will have a negative impact on your proposal.

Why Would They Want to Work With You?

Proposal writers don't usually ask this question. You have a service you think the client will want, and you have pricing that is attractive, but there's another factor related to winning the proposal – the relationship between you and the client.

This relationship, whether it already exists or is one you're trying to describe through the proposal process, can be an important part of the selection process, whether it's formal or not. Your reputation, the proposal itself, presentations and other interactions will all influence the client during evaluation.

As part of your strategy, identify characteristics of your organization and the way you work that match the client's in a way that makes you a compatible partner. Be careful not to overemphasize 'culture', or simply repeat back what you've read in their Mission, Vision and Value statement or other resources. You need to demonstrate this in a sincere, honest way.

You can include those elements within your proposal response, either directly in the sections or questions, or woven through the entire proposal response in suitable locations. Of course, how you handle the overall process and your approach to communicating with the client before or during the proposal process is important. This includes all levels, right from senior members to administrative assistants.

Use existing clients to demonstrate why the client should want to work with you. Tell stories about issues or events where you worked with the client to solve problems or support them. Be honest about problems, but use them to show how you deal with the clients in a positive way.

Example

Demonstrate your professionalism:

If you lost a client in the past and worked very hard to ensure that the transition to their new service provider went smoothly, use this as an example. Include the client as a reference.

The real test of a relationship isn't when things go well, it's when they don't. Use testimonials where possible. Describe your methods of managing the contract if they will appeal to the client. This could be, for instance, monthly or quarterly visits by your president. You may have other initiatives that speak to relationships, such as annual conferences you hold for clients, where they learn about the latest technologies and services, and you bring together people from various organizations to discuss common issues or other processes.

Of course, to do this well, you need to understand the client. If the client would want attention from senior members of your organization, describe how you do that. If they only want to see your frontline manager, describe that, too. Whenever you describe your approach and processes for interacting with the client, be sure to tell them you're flexible and will adapt to their preferences.

The reason for this is that some clients will want a very hands-off approach and won't want to consult with or be involved in the process they feel they've downloaded to you, while others will prefer much more involvement. The problem is, unless you know which of these scenarios matches the client, you should avoid alienating either one in your proposal response.

Summary

The best RFP proposal speaks directly to the client and their needs, which means a customized response that takes into account the nuances and interests of the client, in addition to describing the solution and benefits. You need to do your research and ensure the evaluators get what they need to give you a high evaluation without much effort.

Techniques You Can Use:

- ✓ Answer the question: Why would they choose you?
- ✓ Use modern techniques to find information you can use.
- ✓ Focus your efforts on what the evaluators need.
- ✓ Give them what they ask for, as well as what they need.

Traps To Avoid:

- ✖ Don't assume you understand the client.
- ✖ Don't ignore the client's needs and give them boilerplate material.
- ✖ Don't just go by what's said in the RFP. Read between the lines.

Your Action Plan to Write Better Proposals:

Based on this chapter, list several things you need to do or must do differently to win more business with your proposals.

Priority	Things to Do

Part 5
If You Can't Sell, Go Home

Whether you like it or not, writing a proposal is all about selling. The purpose of the proposal is to close the deal with the client. It has to sell your capabilities and your benefits through a tough medium – one-way communication that doesn't usually let you counter the client's arguments or resistance about buying your services as is possible with traditional sales calls.

At the same time, clients who issue RFPs are sophisticated and don't expect a hard sales pitch. They need to see details of your proposed solution and evidence of your capabilities, not marketing material.

The selling approach has to be strategic and convince the client that you're the best choice.

Here are three key techniques included in this section:

- Keep the sales fluff out of your proposal.
- Use sales techniques to get your message across.
- Figure out ways to make your message stick with the evaluators.

> *"The only people in the world who can change things are those who can sell ideas."*
>
> *– Louis Wyse, advertising executive*

Can You Sell What You're Selling?

Responding to an RFP is selling, so you need to be able to sell your services to be successful. It's a sophisticated audience, however, so the traditional sales and marketing pitch won't work. An RFP has a very specific purpose so it requires a very different approach.

The key is to differentiate yourself from the competition, and clearly demonstrate to the client why you should be selected. This is done by following the requirements, and providing information, details and evidence that will get you the highest score on the evaluation.

Unfortunately, just providing the facts isn't enough either. The client won't read the facts and translate those into why they should select you. You need to tell them and help them make the connection.

Toot your own horn, but don't use a bullhorn

An important part of the proposal is selling your product or service. Proposals that don't sell are often written by professional writers who don't understand the business, and haven't been given sufficient guidance by the company to properly position the information. They're also written by subject matter experts or subcontractor staff who are intimately involved in the details of the service and so enthusiastic about what they do that they feel this in itself should sell and that all they need to do is provide information and technical descriptions.

The reality is that you must sell your service in a proposal – you won't win with a well-written document that only provides raw details and facts about the service, but doesn't sell your services. That said, a proposal that sells to the extreme yet doesn't contain information, facts and evidence to support what's being said, won't win either.

Lessons Learned

Don't over-sell or you may fall flat:

A company that recently changed their name billed themselves as the 'next generation' of service providers. When questioned about the benefits of their 'next generation' service, they weren't able to truly differentiate themselves. Their words did not match reality.

To win your proposal, you must link your features with the benefits to the client. This includes, where possible, the unique selling points of your service. Be careful not to overdo it or it will sound like a marketing and sales pitch, and you may even come across as arrogant.

The best way to sell is subtly, by pointing things out in your services, technology, staff, procedures and experience that support your claims that you provide a benefit. Do this throughout the proposal and don't be afraid to repeat the key benefits when the opportunity arises. Be sure to be consistent in the wording and terminology you use throughout the proposal.

Tip

In the book *Words That Work,* Dr. Frank Luntz identifies consistency and repetition as an effective way to get your message across.

Match what you say with the scoring matrix and evaluation criteria, even using some of the same wording. This will make it much easier for the evaluator to link your statements with the scoring criteria. Ultimately, your key audience is the people scoring your proposal.

Differentiate yourself

While selling your benefits is important, you also need to differentiate yourself from your competition.

Often, people writing proposals focus on what they're capable of doing and don't relate that to their competition. Since most proposal evaluation comes down to comparing you with your competition either directly or by scoring against pre-established criteria, the ability to differentiate yourself from the competition to get a better score will help you win.

Tip

In *The 22 Immutable Laws of Marketing* by Al Ries and Jack Trout, the 14th law of marketing is the law of attributes.

The authors say that marketing is a battle of ideas, and that for every attribute, there's an effective opposite attribute.

Understand your attributes and the competition's opposing attributes. Use this knowledge when you write about your attribute in the proposal.

With research and analysis, you should understand what the client does and doesn't care about. Some of that may be clear in the evaluation criteria, but there will be other factors you can't simply read about in the RFP document.

Differentiating yourself can be as simple as stating your background and experience as it relates to the service, and the differences between you and your competitors in how you deliver.

Your differentiators may be technology, including systems and integration or electronic billing, deeper expertise in certain aspects of the service, the location of your offices, personnel, quality system ISO registration, unique processes, geographic coverage, size, etc. But don't waste your time listing all the ways you're different, simply focus on the differentiators the client actually cares about.

When you find the differentiators and focus on them, make it easy for the evaluators to see how you differentiate yourself, especially where the differentiators relate to evaluation criteria. The evaluators should be able to relate what you're saying to the scoring matrix without digging through your material.

Sell the Steak as Well as the Sizzle

You've heard the saying "sell the sizzle, not the steak". It's a common marketing phrase meant to focus the sales effort on the benefits of a product or service, not the features.

While the concept is right, your proposal needs to focus on the steak as well as the sizzle. Clients are sophisticated buyers and won't be swayed by sales pitches and marketing fluff.

If you just focus on the sizzle, or benefits, you may get interest from the client, but if you can't back it up with substance that demonstrates your track record, technology, resources and your ability to deliver the promised benefit, you won't convince the evaluators. In addition, if you can't quantify the benefit in a way that's meaningful to the client, they may not see the importance of what you have to offer.

Provide substance and concrete information to back up your proposal response. Don't just tell them of the benefits, demonstrate how you can deliver and where possible, use examples as objective evidence of your success and abilities.

Example

Details and evidence support your capabilities:

The Sizzle: Our call center has won an industry service award, and has high reliability with the best trained agents in the industry, skilled at solving issues more often than the industry average.

Add the Steak: We service 34 clients through two call centers, providing a high level of redundancy. Each agent has a minimum two years call center experience with five days of initial training on client products. All supervisors are past service representatives from the client's industry. We benchmark each agent and agents below the benchmark rates are retrained. This high level of quality means there are 20% fewer product returns.

At an estimated 30,000 returns per year, our service saves 6,000 returns or a total of $600,000 in lost revenue for you.

Substance and concrete information should be provided to add the 'steak' to the 'sizzle' for two reasons:

- To support the benefits you propose by providing an actual example with a current or past client, describing past experience, outlining how you accomplish the results and providing facts and figures.
- To provide an example of how the benefit will actually help the client.

It's Not About You – It's About Them

The most important thing to remember about writing a proposal is that it's all about them – the client – not about you. What this means is the proposal itself has to be focused on the client and their needs, not you and your capabilities. This is a fine distinction, but will make a big difference in your final proposal.

Look at everything you do in the proposal and make sure it's focused towards the client requirements and what their expectations are – not what you think they need or what your writers and subject matter experts think is most important.

This can come across in many very subtle ways, including not referring to your company name too frequently.

Lessons Learned

Make it about the client, not you:

In one RFP response, the supplier started almost every paragraph with their own name, along the lines of 'We will,' 'We provide,' 'We are,' and 'We have.'

The supplier should have started more paragraphs with a reference to the customer and their problem, then how they (the supplier) can solve it.

Don't focus too much on your service. Turn it around and discuss the client's problems and show how your service solves their problem. In other words, sell the solution or benefit your service provides, not the details and features of the service. Don't make the client have to work to link your service to the solution they need. If you can't write it clearly in your proposal, they may not see it.

In a sense, you need to feel their pain. Just being a bystander won't give you the insight you need for a winning proposal. You need to fully understand where they're coming from and respond to them directly. This may involve putting aside your 'insider' view of the service you deliver and understand how the client views it.

Ghosts Can Lead to Success

You write a proposal to demonstrate that you're better than your competitor, but it's not appropriate to say negative things about your competition or their services.

Ghosting is a term for trashing your competitors without trashing them directly. With a good understanding of the differences between you and your competitor and how these will look to the client, you can use subtle techniques that get the client to look closer at the competitor's claims and to doubt some of them.

When describing the benefits of your technology, approach, processes and resources, you can provide a direct comparison to illustrate your point. The comparison may just happen to be something your competitor thinks is a benefit. If they haven't described their benefits as well as you have, you may be able to convince the client not only that yours is superior, but that theirs is a risk.

Example

This language was used to 'Ghost' much larger competitors, some of whom are national, with a smaller client:

"We have focused on regionally-based clients instead of spreading resources across the country. Our client base is large enough to provide exceptional economies of scale and low costs without stretching nationally to the point that each client becomes just a line item in the profit and loss statement."

You can use this in every aspect of your proposal, but use it carefully. Don't ever mention the competition since you don't want to acknowledge them or have the client see that you're putting them down directly. You want it to be more subconscious.

The more you know about your competition and the client's needs, the easier this will be. Focus on areas where you're different and see whether you can ghost them on those differences. List the benefits or attributes you have and the ones they have, and then see if you can flip theirs into negatives.

If done well, you could even turn what your competitor might think is an advantage into a disadvantage while deflecting their ghosting efforts. The idea is to plant the seed of doubt in the reviewer's mind.

Another way to do this is by including a checklist of features and related benefits or even risks. You can do this with your technical solution, your systems, processes resources, experience, etc. Expand the list to include features you don't have but your competition does have, and identify the risks or even the benefits if they aren't as compelling as your benefits. This not only gets your message across, it makes it easy for the reviewers to think about the differences between you and your competition – crafted to benefit you, of course.

Example

Consider how you compare to other market solutions:

For instance, if your system is developed and maintained in-house, you can quantify the benefits over an off-the-shelf solution used by your competitor. The competitor will also do the same in reverse, so think about the benefits their approach has and what they may say about yours, and be sure to counter those points.

When you're using this process, you need to think about the evaluation mechanisms and processes being used on the RFP. When you understand the approach, you can better position the ghosting.

If the proposals are being compared against each other, your ghosting efforts should influence the relative scores. In many large, formal RFPs, reviewers look at each individual proposal one at a time, and come up with their score using a matrix that ranks you against a standard or expectation. Since there will be more than one reviewer, the other reviewers will start with a different proposal, so it doesn't matter what order they do it in, the results will even out. Simply ensure that when they get to yours, the reviewers will either adjust your score upwards relative to the ones they just reviewed, or adjust the next ones they review down based on your information. While the evaluators may intend to evaluate each proposal on its individual merits, they're human and your ghosting will impact their scoring.

Making Your Message Stick

When writing the proposal, you're trying to ensure the evaluators see the messages you want them to see, remember what they've read, and relate it to their evaluation scoring and criteria to give you a higher score than your competition.

It's not good enough to have the best solution, you need to convince the evaluators in a way that sticks by developing your proposal to maximize the impact.

Tip | Chip and Dan Heath discuss six ways to make your message stick in their book *Made to Stick.*

For proposal writing, these four are the most relevant: Simplicity, Concreteness, Credibility and Stories.

It's not good enough to just get your message across and ensure the reviewers have a positive impression of your solution or experience in your approach.

The reviewers need to remember your message when they conduct their evaluation and also when they have to justify or support their decision, especially when the process involves the evaluators making a consensus decision or developing an average scoring. An evaluator with a vivid memory of your benefits and attributes will be an asset to you.

There are several fundamental ways you can make sure your message sticks in the minds of the evaluators:

Keep it simple

People remember simple things easier than complicated, complex ideas and information. By keeping your language simple and using familiar terms, your message will be easier to absorb. Many proposal writers feel the need to use complex sentences, fancy language and long paragraphs because they believe they'll sound smarter. The reality is that while the evaluators could understand and absorb the information you present this way, they simply won't. They don't have the time or energy, and they have other proposals to read. Simple and clear messages are the ones they remember.

Keep it real

The temptation is to use marketing and sales language that's rich in concepts, promises and theoretical benefits. While that sounds good to the marketing and sales people, and makes the proposal easier to write, it doesn't mean much to the evaluators. They're used to seeing promises and empty statements. What will get the evaluator's attention are real examples and actual situations that illustrate and demonstrate you've done what you say and that they will receive the same benefits. Skip the hyperbole and marketing fluff and provide examples, facts and figures. Without the high pressure sales pitch what you're saying will be more meaningful and memorable.

Keep it honest

The client is a lot smarter and more aware than you may think. Not only do they understand the service they're procuring through the RFP, they probably know the bidders and what they can really do, and they're reading the proposals from your competition. Don't make promises that you and the client know won't be kept, don't make statements that aren't backed up by fact, and if there's an outstanding issue, bring it up and resolve it rather than hope they don't know about it. By doing all this, the client will me more likely to believe what you say.

Make it relevant

What you say will have a greater impact and be more likely to be remembered if you back it up with relevant examples and stories that are directly linked to what you're saying in the proposal.

Rather than simply describing benefits in general terms, find an example you can talk about. When you combine your statement with an experience, you're not only giving your statement credibility, you're providing a relevant experience the client can relate to. Look for linkages between the client, the proposal and your experience. If you can link things together, your message will be more powerful.

If you tell the client a story about how you solved a problem or delivered services, your assertion that you're the best will stick with them because you link your statement to a real story.

When the evaluators can relate to what you're talking about and position that within their own needs and experience they will be better able to remember what you've said, which will influence their evaluation.

Mirroring

This is a very important technique to use when writing a proposal. It helps the evaluators see, retain and use information they have read in your proposal during the evaluation phase. In other words, it's a subtle but effective sales technique.

We've discussed the importance of speaking directly to the client and making it easy for them to evaluate your submission. Mirroring uses key phrases, terminology, issues and facts that are readily identifiable and already used by the client. By doing this you help the client focus on the information you're providing by using the same terminology used by them.

Be careful to use mirroring moderately. Rather than mirroring back to the client a whole phrase used by them, pick out the key words or re-arrange the phrase slightly to fit the context. This technique works better when the client doesn't see it as a technique, and appears natural.

Tip In *Yes!: 50 Scientifically Proven Ways to Be Persuasive*, a study revealed that the use of the mirroring technique on restaurant customers significantly increased the tip food servers received.

Some of the food servers simply listened to the customer's orders and wrote them down. Another group of food servers listened to the order, wrote it down and then repeated the order back to the customer word-for-word to confirm the order.

The food servers who repeated the customer's orders back to them increased the size of their tips by almost 70 percent. This demonstrates the power of mirroring that you can use in your proposals.

As part of the mirroring process, you can take information from background material provided to you by the client, or that you have learned during a site tour, bidders meeting or research. By taking good notes and recording key phrases and concepts used by the client, you can go beyond using the RFP material to successfully mirror the client in your proposal. This can even mean incorporating real issues or examples they identify in your own examples and description of how your services will provide benefits.

Assess and Target the Evaluators

Since your written proposal is the only way to get your message across, and the evaluators take the message and translate it into an evaluation score, the primary focus should be to write for the evaluators.

To do this, speak their language and speak directly to them. Focus on issues and information that will matter to them, not what you like and are comfortable with. Use examples they can relate to and avoid jargon they won't understand.

If you've done your research, you'll have an idea of who the evaluators are or whom they represent within the client organization, and you'll be able to understand what their interests and issues are. The next step is to determine exactly how to get their attention in your proposal. After all, you can't influence someone unless you know what will influence them.

Even the best ideas fail unless you communicate them effectively. This isn't an easy task, but by carefully considering the evaluators' interests beyond the evaluation criteria and scoring matrix, you can tailor your proposal for maximum effectiveness.

Consider how the reviewer will receive each element of your proposal. This includes the level of detail, type of information, tone, wording, and even the message. Keep in mind that this may have to span across different evaluators with different interests. By understanding how your proposal response will be evaluated by the client, you can target the reviewers. Where there is more than one evaluator, which is often the case with large RFPs, write your proposal with more than one audience in mind.

Tip

If reviewers are from different departments or have different interests, you can create headings in each of your answers that include information they're interested in, such as 'Operational Benefits', 'IT Benefits,' or 'Maintaining Quality Control.'

By doing this consistently with the right heading, each reviewer will be able to easily find the information that matters to them throughout your proposal response.

Ask Yourself Critical Questions for Success

Proposal writers are often so focused on the mechanics of responding to the proposal, assembling all the information, getting agreements and ensuring they're compliant with the RFP, that they fail to ask the following key questions.

Does my proposal solve the client's problem?

Clients ask for proposals because they have a problem that needs to be solved. The problems may not be apparent, but at the root of every proposal there's a problem that needs to be solved. You must think about the proposal in terms of the problem, and respond to it as a solution.

You need to know what the problem is, yet the client may not position the RFP as a problem, or even see it in those terms. The proposal response is your opportunity to demonstrate how you can solve the client's problem anyway.

Always frame the RFP in terms of a problem and develop your response so that it describes the problem and provides your solution. If you're certain about the problem being solved, you can state it up-front in the introduction. If you're not certain about what the client sees as the problem, or it may be a sensitive issue, leave it silent and deal with the issue discretely within your proposal response.

Have I differentiated myself from my competitors?

RFPs are essentially a contest between you and your competition. Even if the process generally assesses each proposal separately on its own merits against a defined set of criteria, the comparisons between the separate proposals will always play a part in the evaluation.

While it's important to focus on the evaluation criteria and demonstrate that you meet or exceed it, you should write the proposal to encourage a favorable comparison with your competition. There are subtle ways to differentiate yourself from your competition. Your analysis about the client will identify issues that need to be addressed, and how to differentiate yourself by addressing those items.

When trying to differentiate yourself from your competition, don't make it obvious. Say just enough to enable the client to figure it out, by using language that makes the client think about the differences, and connect the dots between your benefits and strengths relative to your competition.

If I were the client, why would I select my proposal over other proposals?

While you're working on your proposal, constantly ask *'why us?'* If you continually ask this question, you'll start to see the material you've written or the material contributed by others in a completely new light. Thinking about that question will help you eliminate fluff and generalities, and help you focus on details and solid information that the client wants to see.

If you can't easily answer this question for each section or each RFP question you answer, rethink your strategy and what you've written. The only way to win is to give the client reasons to choose you. If you haven't built a compelling case, your competition probably has.

Answer the Question the Client Doesn't Ask

Responding to RFPs always involves answering questions posed by the client, but the real questions you need to answer may have been left unasked:

- Why is what you're telling us better than your competition?
- Why should it matter to us?

So much energy is spent on answering the client's questions or providing the information required by the RFP documents that these two fundamental questions are often overlooked. Yet they are key tools that allow you to sell yourself to the client, and should be answered for each and every question or section of the RFP response.

If you have a hard time answering these questions, you haven't done a good enough job responding to the questions in the first place. In this case, you should go back and figure out what value you provide to the client, and rewrite your answers.

Do You Adapt to the Proposal Style?

How you approach each proposal should be based on the specific nature of the proposal and the client. This ranges from large, formal RFPs, to sole-source proposals.

In a formal RFP, the client usually outlines exactly what they expect in sections you need to cover or questions you need to answer. They'll also identify evaluation scoring and criteria, which guides you in how you respond.

In less formal proposal responses, the structure will be more open and flexible, leaving you to decide how to respond. Hopefully the client will have identified the evaluation criteria that will guide your response, but even if they haven't, you need to consider how the client may evaluate your proposal and respond appropriately.

The information you received formally or informally about the requirements should be incorporated into the proposal response. For an informal proposal, your knowledge about the client should tell you whether they're looking for a long, detailed response, or a short proposal. If you aren't sure, simply ask what they expect. Even if the client knows you very well, put enough detail into your proposal to help support their decision when they accept your proposal.

Adapting to formal RFPs

Formal RFPs are most commonly used for complex services, particularly ones, which have a significant cost over the life of the contract. Many government and institutional organizations use this approach on a broader basis to demonstrate transparency and fairness in their procurement practices. The cost to the client in managing a large, formal RFP process can be considerable, as is the cost for companies who respond to them.

The RFPs can be very different in how they're structured and in how much information they provide to guide your response.

Many RFPs provide an extensive list of questions on a wide variety of subject areas related to the delivery of service. As a result, it's important to follow a rigid format and structure, and respond specifically to the questions.

Example

Usually, the higher the value of the work, the more extensive the RFP is:

For a service with a national scope and a five-year term, the client provided an extensive RFP with detailed service volume information, and scope with a long list of very specific questions on very clear aspects of the service required, including different sections for experience and the proposed approach in each area. These areas included transition-in, proposed project team, technology, human resources, service procedures, innovation, quality assurance, personnel, solving issues, coordination with other suppliers, transition-out, etc.

In a highly-structured RFP, getting additional messages and information across to the reviewer means using creativity and finding the right place to position the information so it fits the questions yet conveys the message.

Some proposal writers are tempted to change things to fit their boilerplate material or the structure they're familiar with, however this is a very risky and short-sighted approach. If the client has asked for specific things in a defined structure, there's a reason. By not following their structure, you risk failure.

Other RFPs don't provide much information – they may just have a few bullet points, which represent the topics to be evaluated, along with a very brief description of the scope.

You have flexibility in how to respond to this type of proposal, yet there's a higher chance of not meeting the client's expectations, since the client hasn't clearly articulated the expectations. While the written response will be challenging, if the scope is fairly open, then your solution and associated cost may also not match the client's needs.

Example

Short RFP's can be more challenging to respond to:

For consulting services, the RFP had just one page describing the scope and expected outcome, and no information on the volumes or any other quantifier to help the bidders understand the level of effort required.

In addition, there were only seven bullets identifying the areas that would be evaluated in the written proposal.

In this case, you need to interpret what the client has asked, and you must decide how to respond to their limited request for information. You must consider what other questions the client might have asked to help you get your message across, and you must include these answers in your response.

In some cases, you may need to get further clarification from the client on their expectations. The client might not realize that their RFP is ambiguous, even if they're quite clear about what they expect. If the ambiguity remains, try proposing several options with different pricing.

These two very different types of RFPs demonstrate why your proposal response should be based on the nature of the proposal itself. You cannot use a cookie-cutter approach to proposals.

Tip

Sometimes, the lack of information is intentional. It may be skewed towards an incumbent who already has the information.

Adapting to simple quotes

For shorter contracts or lower dollar values, the client will sometimes simply contact three companies and ask for quotes. In this case, you should verify that they're seeking other quotations to compare, and ask about the criteria, if they have any. You should also find out who else they're asking for quotes. Sometimes, they will tell you.

If the client is simply taking the lowest price, your response should reflect this. However, if you feel they may be swayed by a better solution, or if they indicate that price isn't the only consideration, provide a short proposal along with your price, even if the client doesn't ask for one. If price is the only consideration, try providing a core or basic price that will meet the client's basic needs, and provide some additional optional pricing for additional services or higher value service that you believe may be of interest.

Regardless of the criteria, you should still demonstrate why your company is the one that should be chosen to provide services to the client. Use the same concepts you would use with a larger RFP to get your message across, and provide a compelling, but shorter response to the client's request.

In addition, if the scope is verbal and somewhat fluid, you can take the opportunity to propose more than one solution with different pricing as appropriate. This will give you the edge over another company who assumes what the client wants and provides only one price.

You can use a standard template to make it easier and more cost-effective to respond to simple quotations. Just a few well-written pages can get your message across. Most information will be the same for similar services or products, but be sure to always customize the proposal to match the client's needs.

Template Suggestion:

- Reiterate the client's problem/service requirement.
- Briefly describe how you will provide the service.

- Differentiate yourself from your competition by demonstrating your benefits. Position these benefits relative to other companies who provide the same services, but don't talk negatively about them.
- Provide one or more pricing options if possible, along the lines of budget, standard and premium service pricing.

Even when responding to simple quotes, you can increase your chance of winning the business by communicating your benefits clearly, concisely and convincingly.

Adapting to sole source or unsolicited proposals

Both a sole source and unsolicited proposal can be approached with a similar process. The difference lies in how much information you have from the client in the first place, and how much you need to research or assume.

Submitting a sole source or unsolicited proposal is often based on your sales effort with the client and preliminary discussions. In a way, they're the same thing. The difference lies in who initiated the proposal.

Sole source opportunities are usually driven from the client, and often based on a recommendation from another organization or a trusted relationship. In this situation, the client is already interested in working with you. The right solution and a price that the client feels is fair will win the business. It may also mean the client considers you to have a unique position in the market that they don't think can be filled by competitors. If this is a new client, you have an excellent opportunity to provide a solution they need, and develop a strong working relationship.

Tip Some clients may use this approach to get information and ideas from you to implement internally or in order to develop a future RFP, so be cautious about the client's intentions and the level of information you provide.

Unsolicited proposal opportunities are usually driven by your sales effort. During the sales process, you may identify a problem that you can solve and decide you want to provide an unsolicited proposal. Generally, you would tell the client in advance and determine whether they'll be receptive, however in some cases, you may provide a short proposal without getting the client's acceptance in advance. This may result in work, further discussions that eventually turn into work, or when the client eventually does issue an RFP, you're more likely to be invited to bid.

Before you submit your proposal, do some research to find out about the client's procurement policies, especially if the client is a government or institutional organization. There may be a threshold over which they're obligated to get three or more prices, or they may even be required to do a formal tender or RFP process. Under that amount, they may have the freedom to accept a single proposal.

It's important to understand the threshold so you don't waste your effort. Especially if you don't know the threshold, you should provide a quote with options or that is easy to adjust with scope changes to bring the total below the threshold. Often the client you're working with is looking for a simple solution that can be implemented without the time and effort of a formal procurement exercise.

If the client has asked for a sole source proposal, ask them if they have a budget in mind. If they share their budget, you're more likely to develop a solution that fits. If their budget is too low, you can let them know it's unrealistic and avoid the effort.

Many of the same principles of responding to a formal RFP will apply, however you get to decide what information to provide and what questions to answer.

Getting information is harder, however, since it isn't provided in an RFP. You need to have a clear idea of the client needs, and a way to extract this from them based on discussions. You can still use the same sources, however, including the web, past employees, annual reports, news releases, etc. The more information you have about the client and their requirements, the more successful your proposal will be, even an unsolicited one.

You need to have some discussions with the client directly. You may already have some information, but you can always use more. Don't be shy about calling the client and asking probing questions. This demonstrates interest and provides you with better direction so you can submit a proposal that meets their needs and expectations. It's the only way you can be sure of what the client wants, since the client hasn't provided that information to you in a bid document.

Two key parts of the proposal are the technical solution and the pricing. In this case, you need to decide what kind of pricing to provide. You can bundle everything up and provide a single price, or you can provide pricing that allows the client to manage the price by deciding on the scope itself. If anything, this will also enable you to get to the table and have a discussion to negotiate and finalize the key things the client wants, as well as the related pricing.

You have a lot more freedom and flexibility with the types of information you provide in the proposal. Instead of following an RFP, which has a series of questions, you have the opportunity to pose your own questions.

Approach this in the form of questions the client may have asked, and answer them in your proposal.

Use the same writing style, structure and approach that you would use in a large-scale RFP, but on a much smaller scale.

Suggested approach:

- Gather information from the client.
- Establish a solution, along with scope and a simplified work plan.

- For sole source:
  - Submit the proposal informally without pricing to your prospective client to gain interest and refine your scope/solution.
  - Modify your proposal based on input and add pricing.
  - Resubmit.
- For unsolicited:
  - Submit your proposal with pricing options.
  - Follow-up.

Suggested content:

Even a sole-source proposal should be put together with as much effort as a competitive proposal. While they're not comparing you against other bidders, if you don't demonstrate that you can do a good job in the proposal, the client may question your ability to deliver. It also provides the context for your pricing and a way to verify exactly what you will deliver for the price.

Here are a few suggested elements you should include in your proposal. The length and depth will depend on the complexity of the service and solution you're proposing.

- **Existing Situation** – Describe what you know about the existing situation in a way that helps shape the solution.
- **Project Objectives** – Reiterate the reasons for the project, usually based on what the client has told you. You can include the risks or negative consequences of not proceeding with the proposal in order to add a sense of urgency and minimize the possibility that it doesn't proceed.
- **Scope of Work** – This is an important part not only to tell the client what you will do, but also to define your level of effort or specifications for the price you submit. It can be used as a reference tool later if there is disagreement. If there are variable items, identify them here.

- **Deliverables** – This is the end product you'll deliver to the client. It may be a report, a completed project, a product, or another tangible. Where possible, quantify what you'll provide so there's no ambiguity or false expectations.
- **Work Plan** – Provide a work plan that includes the steps you'll take, the time you estimate, both in duration and labor hours/days if appropriate, and the involvement, if any, from the client. This can be useful for a service and can provide the basis for the client to suggest changes that bring the proposal in-line with their budget, if necessary.
- **Timelines** – Identify the anticipated start and end date for the work, including final delivery. If there are limits or situations outside of your control, identify them.
- **Fees** – Provide your fees, along with payment terms and extra billing, such as travel expenses.
- **Next Steps** – Clearly identify that starting the work is in the client's hands, and give them a simple engagement form to sign and return as a form of acceptance or approval of your process. If signing the form is appropriate to the client's process, they will appreciate the simplicity and convenience. Even if they have a formal process they need to follow, a sample engagement form shouldn't work against you – the client will simply disregard it.

The headings above (Existing Situation, Project Objectives, etc.) are the generic headings typically used in proposals. Consider formatting your proposal with questions or statements instead of generic headings. Use headings such as:

- Why You Need Our Services
- How You Can Succeed With Us
- What Needs To Be Done
- What You Will Get From Us
- How We Will Do It
- When We Will Start and Finish

- The Value We Provide
- How To Get Started

These new headings cover the same information as the generic titles, however they're much more descriptive and action-oriented.

Summary

Your proposal has to sell without fluff. Use strategy and your understanding of the client to build facts and information that sell without the marketing hype, but make sure your message comes across, and your unique benefits differentiate you from the competition.

Techniques You Can Use:

- ✓ Use Ghosting to deal with your competition's advantages.
- ✓ Make your message stick so it impacts the evaluation.
- ✓ Differentiate yourself from the competition.

Traps To Avoid:

- ✖ Don't start writing until you know how to sell your services.
- ✖ Don't include marketing hype and fluff in your proposal
- ✖ Don't just sell the sizzle, also include the steak.

Your Action Plan to Write Better Proposals:

Based on this chapter, list several things you need to do or must do differently to win more business with your proposals.

Priority	Things to Do

Part 6
It's All About the Content

The content is what your proposal is really about, and it's what the client wants to see when they read it. Good content that answers the questions and demonstrates your capabilities makes it more likely that you'll convey your message and sell your benefits.

Build your content with facts and examples that will be meaningful to the reviewers, and not only support your technical and financial proposal, but also match the evaluation criteria and scoring matrix.

Here are some of the techniques useful for developing effective content included in this section:

- Include facts and examples, not promises and theory.
- Focus on content that will win the proposal, and eliminate information that isn't relevant.
- The best content comes from your contributors and subject matter experts.

> *"Beware of the man who won't be bothered with details."*
>
> – *William Feather*

One-Size-Fits-All is Not a Winning Strategy

Many organizations use boilerplate material because it's an easy, expedient way to provide information. Unfortunately, most RFPs ask for different information, and both the client and the needed solution are unique, so boilerplate material won't win business.

Each client and their requirements are different. To effectively sell your service and your company, you need to manipulate and edit your boilerplate material in a way that it becomes specific to the current client's RFP. This is the only way you can incorporate the strategies and approaches that will make the client chose you over your competition.

There may be a few instances where you want sections of your text to be boilerplate with no customization at all, but even this is a lost opportunity. For instance, when introducing your company's background and history, modifying it to touch on things that will matter and be relevant to the client will give you an advantage. Resist the temptation to take the easy approach – you won't win proposals that way.

In addition, you need to closely review all material you use to make sure that information, names, terms and other details from the source are completely eliminated. You don't want to be including information that identifies it as being from somewhere else and not completely original to the client. Don't just do a 'search and replace'. Read the text and edit each instance, including the client name, to suit the context, otherwise you may end up with some awkward text.

Example

Don't make this boilerplate mistake:

In an obvious cut-and-paste, boilerplate material was taken from a different proposal without editing, and included in a new proposal, even thought the context was very different. The language and examples used were clearly from a different proposal.

The other risk you have to watch out for with boilerplate material is obsolescence. Boilerplate material, such as the naming of processes or software systems, might be old and not fit your current corporate strategy, organization, priorities or solutions.

If you use boilerplate material, use it simply as a base, not as the final text. The best place to get this base material is from the most recent proposal you wrote that is most similar to the current one. But don't be a slave to the text. If you have two pages of boilerplate material on a topic that really should be three paragraphs, don't be afraid to bring it down to the size that fits the context of the proposal, either based on its importance within the proposal, interest to this specific client, or page limits.

Maintaining a library of material can be helpful, particularly for answers to questions asked frequently in the RFPs to which you respond. You can avoid using outdated answers by adding the most recent material to the library after each proposal. When using library material, closely look at it in the new context, and modify as necessary. Keep several versions in the library and decide which best fits your new need.

While you need to use boilerplate material with caution, it's easier to adapt something you already have than to write new material from scratch. Just don't let it become a lazy way to respond to proposals. Invest the effort necessary to win, otherwise you're wasting your resources.

Lessons Learned

Maintain a library of material:

A previous customer called, hoping I had some old material we had written for a previous bid because it closely matched a proposal they were currently working on. The customer wanted to use it as base material, but they couldn't find their own paper or electronic copies, and I hadn't kept a copy.

You should also maintain the original source of any graphics, organizational charts, tables, photographs, screen shots or spreadsheets used in past proposals. Keep them in their original format so you can re-edit easily to fit new requirements.

Bigger is Not Better

A thick proposal looks impressive. The traditional techniques of using lots of boilerplate material and filler will help you achieve a thick proposal, but what's inside will eventually count more in the evaluation.

There's a balance to strike, and it depends on the amount of information the client has asked for and the number of questions they have asked. If the client mandated a fixed maximum page count, it's one less thing to worry about. If they didn't, consider how many pages you need to convey your message without being too onerous for the evaluators to get the information they need to score your proposal.

Lessons Learned

Don't be afraid to eliminate unimportant information:

A 13 page section of the proposal had the key messages and information, but was also filled with other details that were not relevant to the question it was supposed to answer. The evaluators would have had to search to find what they needed to evaluate the answer. It was reduced to 3 pages in the final proposal.

For the Prosecution – It's All About the Evidence

Proposal reviewers automatically assume there will be a certain amount of pure marketing in the proposals they review. You can differentiate yourself and dispel that perception by providing evidence that supports what you've written.

Example

This is generic marketing language that doesn't convince the client:

"Our proposal demonstrates our willing approach to partnering with you to achieve your objectives. Our mission is to align with you in understanding your goals and business plan, working with you in maximizing operating efficiencies and increasing client satisfaction, helping you concentrate on your core business."

Not only is generic marketing language unconvincing, it will lead the reviewers to doubt the validity of your entire proposal if most of what they read is the same type of sales material.

That doesn't mean you can't do a sales pitch, it simply means you need to anchor it in real information and fundamentals, not empty language. You can do this by demonstrating what you say with examples from your past experience, or showing how it will impact specifically on the client, using their own situation as an example.

Saving money, improving services, reducing turnaround time, responding to problems quickly and implementing unique or innovative techniques can be very powerful evidence of what you can do for the client.

You can also include quotes from other clients, or use research and information from other well-known and reputable organizations to support your point.

Example

Use expert sources and independent information to support what you say:

For a proposal response where an innovative and very different approach was proposed as a solution, the company included statistics and references from a well-regarded research organization to give credibility to their approach and satisfy concerns they knew would be raised by the client during the evaluation process.

The ability to provide evidence that demonstrates and supports what you are proposing in a concrete way is an important part of your strategy to increase your credibility and differentiate yourself from your competition. Start to source the supporting information early in the process, and make it a requirement of the proposal contributors. When you see an area of the proposal that doesn't have credible evidence to support it, find evidence and include it in the proposal.

Getting this evidence from within your own organization can be hard. The people you talk to often can't think of solid examples or evidence, and even if they do, they often don't remember or recognize the examples as being relevant. Clearly outline your intent and the purpose of the information you're trying to gather, and interrogate subject matter experts to draw it out. It's often compelling and powerful once you find it.

So, What Have You Done For Me Lately?

A typical RFP approach has the client asking for your experience delivering the service in the past, and how you will deliver the service for them. The questions can be structured in two completely separate sections, one with questions related to your experience, and another with questions related to your approach to delivering services. The RFP may also be structured with two parts for each question, one part asking about your experience and the other about your approach.

Even if the client doesn't ask about your experience, you should include your past experience and how it relates to the current requirements to demonstrate a track record and provide evidence about your abilities.

There's a very good reason clients ask for both your past experience and your approach going forward. While past performance is no guarantee, a track record and experience with the services provides information to the client that enables them to make a more informed decision. It also supports your proposed approach to delivering the service for them, lowering the risk to the client and helping them justify their decision. It's similar to hiring an employee. What they've done to get results for their past employers is an important part of the hiring process and decision-making.

Sometimes your past experience is asked for on a project or client basis within a specific section where you're asked to identify past projects and describe your experience. Usually these are projects very similar in nature to the requirements of the current client.

Even if the client asks for project examples, don't rely on this to get your message across. You should still identify your past experience throughout the proposal when describing the approach you would take with the client, and highlight your success and how you adapt your processors from past experiences to serve new clients. This is done to reinforce that you have experience and an excellent track record not only in providing that service, but also in applying your past experience to meet the unique needs of a new client.

You can also demonstrate experience through resumes. If you've been asked to provide resumes, it's a great opportunity. If you haven't been asked, you should consider including them where appropriate. Don't simply include resumes in job-search format. Rewrite the resumes to be consistent, focus on past work that matches the client needs and background, discuss results and demonstrable performance, and keep it short.

Usually the last thing the client wants to hear is that one-size-fits-all and that they're exactly the same as your other clients. Even clients in the same sector or same line of business consider themselves unique. Your proposal needs to address their unique quality, and describe how you're going to take that unique quality and build it into service you deliver to them.

Answer the Damn Question!

It's a simple concept, yet proposal writers frequently don't answer the question the way the client intended. There are a number of reasons for this. In some cases the writers don't want to answer the question because they may not have an answer. They may not be able to demonstrate how they would do something, how their service is superior or how their experience meets client expectations. They may not have the details they need, the answer isn't likely to satisfy the client, or they don't fully understand the question. Finally, the writers may simply have run out of time.

Rather than thinking you can avoid the issue by not directly answering the question, you need to clearly and effectively answer it. The client will always see through an evasive answer. The result of not answering the question is a lower score and reduced credibility.

Lessons Learned

Just answer the question:

When writing a major proposal for a company early in my career, the president of the company reviewed the proposal periodically and provided comments. One key area was revised several times based on his comments, and yet clearly we had still not met the mark. The president's last comment, written in red on the paper, was "just answer the @#!&*$% question."

This mantra has stuck with me, and it's something I now look for when helping organizations write proposals, or when I review proposals.

Even if you need to admit something you may not want to, such as a lack of experience in a certain area, you need to do it. In Part 3, we discussed how to overcome lack of experience and the importance of admitting issues rather than avoiding them. The bottom line is that you need to respond to every question fully and completely.

Don't miss the point of the question accidentally, either. Pay attention to the tense. When the client asks what you did in the past, don't provide them with your future approach.

Example

They asked for a reason:

When an RFP asked for the names of individuals with authority to sign-off on design documents, the respondent provided the names of subcontractor companies, not the individuals themselves.

The client likely wanted to match the names with the resumes to ensure credentials matched levels of responsibility.

One simple reason the question sometimes doesn't get properly answered is that the question isn't referred to when the answer is written. It may be in a different document and looked at once before the writer started writing the answer, or shortened to become a proposal heading. Reduce this problem by including the actual question right before the answer within the document.

Lessons Learned

Give the writers the full question:

In a failed proposal response, a number of the answers were not complete. The answer matched the question quoted in the proposal itself, but the original questions from the RFP were very long and multi-part. The bidder had edited down the question in their proposal document.

The writer must have read only the edited question and not realized they weren't answering the full question.

With the full question in the proposal document, you won't lose sight of the full question that's been asked. If it's a long, wordy question, as some tend to be, break it apart into its separate sub-questions. Each of these sub-questions should be answered explicitly within the response with their own heading. Not only does this ensure you've answered the question, it makes it easy for the reviewer to score your response and understand what you're saying, because you're responding directly to what they've asked.

A Picture is Worth More Than 1,000 Words

Pictures, meaning graphs, flow-charts, illustrations and other graphics, will help you get your message across in a more meaningful way than a long written section in your proposal.

Since writing a proposal is about getting your message and the related information across, well-made graphics help the reviewer visualize the messages and information in a more concise manner. Don't just add graphics to fill space, break up blocks of text, or simply to look good. Graphics must have a purpose to be effective.

While graphics usually can't stand on their own, adding good graphics reduces the amount of text you need, and enables the reviewer to visualize what you're saying by simplifying complex information. This results in a better understanding of your point, and better retention when it comes to evaluation time.

Using graphics is particularly useful if you have a page limit. Often, using shorter text and explanations coupled with a well thought-out and well-drawn graphic gets your point across in much less space.

Make sure your graphic does get the point across and is not too complicated. Common software programs, such as Microsoft's PowerPoint, provide an easy method of developing diagrams of various types. While they can be helpful, you don't need to have specialized graphics programs to achieve good results. Use what you have, and ensure your graphics are appealing and effective.

When developing complex graphics to illustrate your point, have somebody who is not familiar with the proposal and the details behind the graphic review it (and related text) to get their impression. If they can clearly see what your intention is with the graphic, use it. If not, go back to the drawing board and rethink it.

For graphics of any kind, always keep the original source files in their editable format, and save them in a non-editable graphic format for insertion into your document.

Your graphics should be small enough to include in the main body of your proposal rather than in an appendix. If something is complex enough that it needs to go into the appendix because of size, you need to also produce a simplified version to include in the main body.

Graphics can be small or large, and they can support or replace text. Either way, they're a much more effective way of getting across the message, while also creating visual interest and breaking up what might otherwise be large blocks of text.

Don't Put Too Much Junk in the Trunk

It's tempting to include a lot of extra content in the appendix with the belief that the more information you provide, the more convincing it will be.

Frequently, a reference within the proposal directing the reviewer to the appendix is all that's provided.

Whether the reviewer bothers to read the appendix or not is out of your hands, so the material may not even be seen. Even if it is, it may be too detailed for some reviewers, so they won't learn what you want from it. Turning to the appendix also interrupts the flow of your proposal and the flow of information, making the message you're trying to get across harder to absorb, especially since the reviewer has to leave the main proposal. Also, the reviewer may review the appendix after reading the main proposal, in which case the context will be lost.

First, carefully consider whether the material needs to be put into an appendix. If it is, be sure to provide an introduction in the main body that includes the points you're trying to make with the appendix material. Include a summarized or short version in the main body as well.

Example

Don't rely on the appendix:

If you include a detailed flowchart in the appendix, for instance, summarize it on one page in the main body, and provide a written commentary. Hit on the main points and items that specifically interest the client. Evaluators will get what they need out of the one page summary. Evaluators who are interested may also look at the appendix to see the details and evidence you provided to demonstrate your message.

Gantt charts

Gantt charts and project timelines are often long and detailed, even requiring a different page orientation or size to make them large enough to read. Even if you include these charts in the main body of the proposal, create a one-page summary of the timeline with key milestones identifying the start and end-date of the project to match up with the client's needs. Frame the charts with an introduction and bullet points explaining some of the key elements of your schedule and the benefits to the client. This will generally satisfy most reviewers, and show them that you've covered the requirements. The details, if required, can be provided in the appendix, particularly if a detailed schedule is a requirement of the RFP. In the meantime, you've provided relevant messaging around your schedule within the main body of your text.

Resumes

When resumes are required as part of the submission, they're often added to the appendix, either by choice or because the RFP has instructed that they be included there. This is a good place for traditional resumes, which are too long to include in the main body of the proposal.

To get the best value out of the information, include at least a one-paragraph summary and bullet points with the relevant information for key resumes you include. This way, you'll clearly identify the key strengths, experience and benefits of the team member as part of your proposal without the reviewers having to read the full resume and trying to connect it with their needs. You should make it easy for the reviewers, and provide a clear connection.

When writing the summary and bullet points, consider the issues, hot buttons and themes, and pull forward the elements that matter to the reviewer and match the evaluation criteria.

Even if you provide shortened resumes within the main body, start them off with a quick summary that gets across the message.

Large documents

Manuals, policies and procedures are sometimes asked for in RFPs to demonstrate that you actually have the material you claim you have and to see what you've done for other clients.

Even if they aren't requested, sometimes these documents can be useful to include as proof of your experience or expertise, depending on your concerns over proprietary information. If you include this type of document, include it in the appendix, but also add the Table of Contents (or a shortened summary version) within the main body of the proposal along with an explanation of the key benefits, where they're currently used, how you update them on a regular basis, how you will adapt to individual client requirements and other key messages you want to get across to the reviewer. Simply referring the reviewers to the appendix without positioning the content will waste an opportunity to demonstrate your benefits.

If you don't want to include your proprietary documents in the appendix, include just the Table of Contents and a summary of the document. Tell them what it's for and describe the contents that are particularly relevant, how you will use them and, if necessary, how you will adapt them to the client's needs.

Specification sheets

If you need to include detailed information about products or standard sales material about a process or service, use the same strategy as for large documents unless otherwise requested by the RFP, and include the specifications and product information in an appendix. Summarize the key elements or the key benefits that are of interest to the client in the main body.

It's not useful to simply refer the reviewer to the appendix for more information. You must set the stage with an introduction or summary, identifying the key attributes and selling points within the main body before sending the reviewer into another part of the proposal document. Consider the flow of information and making it easy for the reviewer to easily get the information they need to evaluate you without being distracted.

Get Rid of the Clutter

Your proposal is meant to persuade by getting your message across to the reviewer. If your message is hidden, the reviewer may not see it. Often, the most important information is buried inside other information that is much less relevant. This makes it hard for the reviewer to match your proposal with the evaluation criteria.

Look at everything you include in your proposal and prioritize. You may find some things that are important to you and the subject matter experts aren't important to the client, or that some information isn't strong enough to influence them. That doesn't mean eliminating that material. You can relocate it to the appendix and provide a summary in the main body, or you can restructure your response to ensure the most important information is provided up-front or in a more obvious way. It's a careful balance when deciding what you should and shouldn't include, but you must have the courage to eliminate material that doesn't advance your message.

They Didn't Ask? Tell Them Anyway!

Many RFPs have a very structured approach, which you need to follow in your response, including the specific set of questions you must answer. There may be other things the client didn't ask about, but it's to your advantage to give them an answer anyway.

Based on your analysis of the client, or based on your competitive advantage, you may have issues or information you would like to put forward but the client hasn't asked for them and it isn't part of the formal evaluation or scoring criteria.

Ask yourself whether adding the information will positively influence the scoring and evaluation of your proposal. If it will, you should consider adding it. If not, then don't distract the reviewers from the parts of the proposal that are necessary for evaluation.

While deviating from the mandated RFP response structure is not usually a good idea, there are creative ways you can get your information across within the structure of the RFP. Analyze the existing questions and the evaluation and scoring matrix to identify areas where your new information can be provided.

Example

Answer their concerns, even if they don't ask:

A company proposing to use a subcontractor answered the question of what their contingency plan was in case the subcontractor couldn't perform – without being asked.

Within the existing responses, you can simply provide your information within the text, under a sub-heading, or add language such as:

- In addition to...
- Another important issue is...
- We are sometimes asked about... and here's how we deal with it.

Depending on the RFP itself and the questions asked, you can find other creative ways of transitioning into answering a question the client has yet to ask, or of adding the information.

Telling Stories

When you respond to the RFP, providing evidence that you're capable and have the experience to do the job is important.

Rather than simply listing examples, turn them into stories and use the details of the experiences and successes throughout your response, weaving it into every area and question possible.

Doing this consistently throughout your proposal using the same related examples will have more impact than using disconnected examples. It helps reinforce the message to the client.

The stories you tell should support your answer, and demonstrate what you've done in the past in a way that benefits the client in a concrete way they can relate to. You can also tell stories about how you have dealt with problems or issues in the past and how you can adapt those experiences to benefit your new client.

Keep in mind that successful experiences aren't just things that went well. Success includes encountering a problem and resolving it. This demonstrates you've learned valuable lessons from your experience, and are able to apply that learning to the client's benefit. As described in Part 4, identifying problems you faced and demonstrating how you're able to solve them is just as important as demonstrating successes.

By telling a story, even if you change the names for confidentiality, the information you provide is more likely to be remembered and will have more impact.

Include your stories into the text itself, or include them in a sidebar. As described in Part 7, using sidebars and boxes for this kind of information is very effective, and is more likely to be absorbed by the reader. It also breaks up the long narrative feel of your text.

Stories are typically used to reinforce the hot buttons, themes and key points you want to stress to the client. By using them this way, you have more impact on the final evaluation of your proposal.

Extracting Material from SMEs and Subcontractors

Getting material from the subject matter experts (SMEs) within your organization, or from subcontractors and suppliers, can be challenging. There are a few reasons for this. Often, these individuals don't know how to write effectively, and may not fully understand what's expected of them. If they're technical experts, their focus and interests may not match what you need to provide. These people are probably passionate about what they do, but don't know how to sell that.

Lessons Learned

Curb their enthusiasm:

A subject matter expert wrote a 13-page description of the company's processes in response to an RFP question. It demonstrated the SME's passion with lots of technical details, but it didn't address the value or benefits to the client. The text was edited down to three pages in the final proposal – key benefits included.

Suppliers or subcontractors may also be busy with their own current business, and not be as focused on the RFP as you.

If your bid requires input from subject matter experts or subcontractors and suppliers, it's important for these individuals to be at the table during the kick-off meeting and subsequent meetings where you discuss strategy and approach in areas that relate to them, as they may not have the full context of the RFP or the overall service. If necessary, hold a kick-off meeting especially for the subject matter experts or subcontractors and suppliers after your main internal meeting.

In addition, provide guidelines and guidance that these individuals can use when writing material. One way to do this is to provide them with a writing template. Not only will this make it easier for you to incorporate their material into your full proposal, it lets you give the writers the sub-questions and headings/topics they need to address so that they are consistent with the rest of the proposal.

Providing style sheets, which provide guidance to the writers on hot buttons, issues, themes, key messages and terminology will also make it easier. By taking this extra effort, you're more likely to receive material that's useable.

The style sheet will also ensure a cohesive and consistent writing style throughout the proposal. The consistency won't be obvious to the client, but inconsistencies will stick out and detract from your proposal.

If your supplier performs a particular portion of the work and the response in your RFP on that service is completely different from the rest of the proposal, the client will wonder how you can work together and provide a consistent and seamless service delivery when you can't even get it right on your proposal. In addition, large changes in style or structure will make the proposal harder to read.

After the material from the subject matter experts is edited, have the experts review the final text, particularly if the work has involved professional writers or other individuals who don't fully understand the material.

Compliance Matrix

There are two types of compliance requirements. The first is the proposal response, which includes providing written information and answering questions. The second is made up of the more technical requirements, which include providing an original signed copy, labeling requirements, acknowledging amendments, providing insurance information, corporate information, etc.

Using a compliance matrix as part of your process will ensure you not only address all the questions and information requirements, but also don't miss a technical requirement that could lead to disqualification. This is essentially a check-off list of the key compliance requirements. Tick off the items as you complete them, and then do it once again when the final proposal is ready to be packaged.

Tip

For any proposal you submit, ask yourself the following questions:

Are you compliant?: Do you meet the minimum and mandatory requirements?

Are you responsive?: Have you answered all questions fully and completely, or if there are no formal questions, have you provided sufficient information for the client to make a decision?

In many cases, the RFP questions or sections become the compliance matrix, with specific elements that are requested becoming part of the response. Your compliance matrix lists each one of these, along with the things you need to include in the answer. Your Red Team can also use the compliance matrix when they review the draft proposal.

For each section, list all the questions, and within each of those questions, identify the information you need to provide, including your quality control methods, past experience, benefits, and any other key information the client has asked for, or you want to convey.

For each question, you may end up with a checklist that looks like this:

Item to be covered	Introduction	Demonstrate we meet the requirements	Specific past experience	Quality management of services	Reporting and benefits	Resources – who will be involved	Interaction with the client	Benefits of our company's services	Summary	Full review complete?
Question 1										
Question 2										
Question 3										

Another type of compliance table you can use are for specific technical requirements, such as things you need to do or submit, including bonding or proof of insurance, for instance, in order to be compliant with the requirements. These items may have an impact on your score or be mandatory requirements. Failure to comply could result in disqualification. Using a compliance matrix to itemize and verify these requirements reduces the possibility of making a mistake.

Some of the items related to key compliance could include:

- ☑ Insurance certificates provided
- ☑ Bonding provided
- ☑ Sign-off of key documents such as confidentiality
- ☑ Signature on the original submission
- ☑ Identifying compliance with security requirements
- ☑ Addenda's acknowledged
- ☑ Providing a pricing sheets as per instructions
- ☑ Labeling and packaging as per directions

Start creating your checklist early. During your review of the RFP as described in Part 3, identify all the requirements and include them in your checklist.

Summary

The content is sandwiched between the strategy and the writing. Content builds on the strategy you developed, and feeds into the writing exercise. The content has to relate directly to the specific client and the specific RFP you're writing, and must contain facts and information that give your message credibility and make it easy for the client to choose you.

Techniques You Can Use:

- ✓ Customize the content to the client for more impact.
- ✓ Answer the questions fully and completely.
- ✓ Use well thought-out graphics to illustrate your message.

Traps To Avoid:

- ✖ Don't use boilerplate material without customizing it for your proposal.
- ✖ Don't assume your contributors will provide what you need.
- ✖ Don't include content that isn't directly relevant to your message.

Your Action Plan to Write Better Proposals:

Based on this chapter, list several things you need to do or must do differently to win more business with your proposals.

Priority	Things to Do

Part 7
Getting it All On Paper

Writing the proposal response itself is usually an iterative process that involves ensuring your message is clear and evident, using the content you developed in the previous section.

Since your proposal interacts with your prospective client through the writing, you must write effectively to demonstrate you're the company best able to provide services. Don't hide your value and capability behind weak writing.

You write your proposal to influence the client. Without good writing, your message will not be clear or convincing.

If you heed the words of your high school English teacher, or use what you learned in a business communications course, you're probably not getting the results you need from your proposals.

You need to go further than technically correct writing. You need to communicate complex information to busy, distracted evaluators.

> *"I didn't have time to write a short letter, so I wrote a long one instead."*
>
> *– Mark Twain*

The Elements of Successful Proposal Writing

There are some basic yet important steps to communicating effectively in your proposal. While you need to adapt the approach to your own situation, the size of your proposal and the type of contributors, the following elements should be incorporated into your writing to make it compelling and convincing:

- ✓ Understand the client and their needs.
- ✓ Be clear about your message, benefits and solution before you start to write.
- ✓ Provide facts and information that support the message.
- ✓ Organize your information so it's easy to see and absorb.
- ✓ Be short and concise – don't make the proposal longer than it needs to be, and don't use long sentences or big words.
- ✓ Consider what the client wants to hear, not just what you want to say.
- ✓ Don't assume too much – spell it out if there's any doubt.

Example

It isn't just pretty writing:

An unsuccessful proposal looked like it had been written by sales or marketing staff, with little if any involvement from the company's operations staff.

The proposal was well written from a literary perspective, but didn't reflect the company's real capability.

What You're Up Against

The evaluators will have a stack of thick proposals to assess, all competing for their attention and capacity to absorb and retain the information with which they need to evaluate you.

Even when focused on the task without external distractions, our ability to absorb large amounts of written material is limited. Not everything will be seen, and not everything will be remembered. The key is to make it as easy as possible for evaluators to see and remember what really matters. It's another reason not to include too much unnecessary information in a proposal.

When it comes to the reviewers, you're fighting against powerful forces that make it difficult to get your message across:

Short attention span

If you don't get the point across quickly, you lose the reviewer's interest.

Information overload

The reviewers are bombarded with information, so your message must be uncluttered and dead simple to see and understand.

Very little time

A long, leisurely read is often out of the question, even if the reviewers could keep focused, so the reviewer will go fairly quickly over most of the material. Dense, hard-to-read material will escape their attention, so use techniques that focus their eyes and attention on the things that matter.

Instead of including unnecessary material and details, or trying to sound smart with long, complex sentence structure, make your proposal short, snappy and easier to read. Don't repeat the same tired formats and text from previous proposals – write the proposal with the details, information and structure that makes it easier for the reviewers.

Strategic writing

Even though you have a proposal response strategy and have collected or developed the content, it still needs to be written in a clear, concise and compelling way that helps the evaluators and increases your chances of winning the RFP.

Similar to the overall proposal, you need to have a strategy specific to your writing before you start.

Tip | *"Communicating without a strategy is like throwing darts blindfolded, it's just less likely to hurt your audience."* - Michel Theriault

Effective writing isn't just putting words down on paper. Your written proposal isn't the proposal itself – it's an interface between the proposal evaluators and your company's technical and financial solution.

Getting this part wrong can help you lose the business. Getting it right will substantially increase your chances. Start with a plan to represent your technical solution and content in a way that makes the information stick in the minds of the evaluators.

7 deadly sins of writing

Here are the 7 deadly sins of writing you need to avoid when writing your proposal:

- ✖ Writing without a plan.
- ✖ Writing what you want to say, not what the audience wants to read.
- ✖ Trying to sound too smart.
- ✖ Writing too much fluff.
- ✖ Following a structure that's hard to read.
- ✖ Making your key message hard to find.
- ✖ Leaving the good stuff for the end.

After you've read this section, go back and look at some of your older proposals or those written by someone else in your organization. You'll probably see many of these mistakes and understand why they don't work.

Avoid Disaster – Start with an Outline

An outline ensures you get all the information you need in the proposal, and that the flow is logical and supports the persuasive nature of your response with a consistent structure between each section or question.

When writing your proposal, start with an overall outline using the content you have and the RFP structure you're following.

The outline ensures you provide the strategic elements you need to win. It identifies where and how to address the hot buttons, issues and themes for each section or individual question. Having your contributors, including subject matter experts or sub-contractors, use the outline, will improve the results you get from them.

If you start writing without an outline, you end up with random, non-cohesive text throughout your entire proposal. You may repeat things you don't need to repeat, and not repeat things you should repeat. You may even forget to include some important information.

An outline helps identify information you have to collect and include in the proposal. This could be examples from your current client base, information about experience and background, key members of your proposal, resumes, samples, and other information, which supports your message.

With an outline, you can have somebody else help you by going through the outline and know exactly what information needs to be collected. They can also start the collection process early so you have the information when you need it.

To create an outline, start at the top. If the RFP has specific questions you have to answer, your outline would start with each of those questions. Next, list the sub-headings to add and then the themes, information, details and messages to include. The more details you have in your outline, the easier will be your overall process.

Example

Good advice in an RFP's instructions:

"The proposal content and structure should be written in the same order, format, numbering and titles as presented in the RFP."

Build in the Message

Your message, including hot buttons, issues and themes, must be carefully integrated throughout the entire proposal, and guide how you structure your content and present the information.

While you have the overall message, consider developing sub-messages on a more detailed level for each of the questions or sections. In addition to the overriding messages, you will find other things in your source material that should be highlighted or described in a specific way to match the evaluation criteria or the key messages you developed earlier.

How Much Should You Write?

The rule of thumb for how long your proposal should be is that it has to be as long as you need to get your point across without overwhelming the evaluators. As indicated earlier, more is not better.

Tip

"... brevity, clarity, and simplicity are simply the hallmarks of good communication." – Dr. Frank Luntz, *Words That Work*

In some proposals, you'll be given a page count limit that forces you to respond within pre-defined limits. This may even include specifying font size and minimum margins. If you're given a page limit, write close to the limit without going over. In some cases, you'll be given page count limits for specific questions or sections.

If no maximum page count is given, take a disciplined approach and make sure you don't write too much. There's a temptation to include all the material you can find. As explained previously, this tendency results in material that is not relevant to the actual evaluation of your proposal and may distract the reviewer from the messages that are most important.

Tip | If you're given a limit, follow it. You'll either be disqualified, or any pages over the limit will simply be discarded before they're seen by the evaluators.

If you aren't given a page count limit, assess what a reasonable limit would be and take a similar approach to page counts for various questions or sections. By providing a page count limit internally while you're developing the proposal response, you're much more likely to get concise information from your internal writers, subject matter experts and subcontractors.

A rough guideline for allocating space is to use the scoring matrix and allocate a page count to specific questions or sections based on their value in the scoring matrix. For instance, if you have a 100 page limit and a specific section is worth 20% of the total score, you would allocate 20 pages to that section. This is only a starting point, since there may be specific areas where you need more or less space to appropriately address the question and provide the required information.

If you assess information and decide whether it's important enough to include during the overall process, the size of your proposal will naturally develop. It's important to take a critical eye and not be afraid to discard, summarize or shorten material that was provided to you by others.

Structure and formatting is discussed later, but don't sacrifice a readable proposal to make a shorter one. Eliminating useful elements that take additional space, such as introductions, summaries, diagrams, bullet points, sub-headings and shorter paragraphs just to trim pages will defeat the purpose of communicating your message.

Write to Communicate

Your writing has to be about strategically communicating information with shorter, tighter, leaner sentences and paragraphs using a light, open format. It doesn't need to be as smooth and conversational as other writing. Make the writing to the point with structure that breaks it up visibly but maintains the flow using more bullet points instead of paragraphs, and more headings to identify key information.

If you can't accomplish this internally, find help. There may be someone in your organization with skills you can borrow, or hire a professional. The job of the professional should be to polish what you produce, unless the professional is intimately familiar with your business. Even then, make sure they understand that you're writing a proposal. They may have a view on writing that's more suitable for a newsletter or annual report.

What will influence them?

Armed with knowledge about the evaluator and the evaluation criteria, you need to consider what information to include and how that information should be presented to influence the evaluators.

If existing service problems are an issue with the client, you can use your track record of service. If cost savings are key, you can propose alternate scope or service approaches to save money without simply cutting the price to the point where service will suffer. If the environment and green issues are prevalent in the client's news releases and public information, focus on your ability to support the client in being a good corporate citizen.

Use the same approach for any other characteristic or issue that you can link to the company or the individuals.

Speak their language

If you have to use acronyms or terms, use the ones the client is likely to be familiar with and even then, spell them out fully, or explain them the first time you use them within a section or question. This is important, as depending on the RFP format, it's possible your proposal will be separated into parts and evaluated by various subject matter experts.

If you need to use terms the evaluators may not be familiar with, explain them when you first use them to ensure the evaluators understand them. For short terms, it may be better to use the full term, not the acronym. When possible, use generic terms instead of proprietary terms. For example, use the generic term for a process or software instead of the name of a specific company's system. If you want to emphasize the value of the specific company's system, do that by explaining its benefits, not by repeating the brand name throughout the proposal.

Tip Use a sidebar on the page to explain an acronym or term where necessary to help the evaluators understand. By keeping these explanations separate from the main text, you won't disrupt the flow.

Be careful when using terms and acronyms that are internal to your organization. If you use terminology, phrases, job titles and other references that are used within your organization but nowhere else, you will have a hard time getting your message across.

Change those references to something the client will understand and is commonly seen in the industry. If necessary, you can include the industry-common terms as well as your terms if it's important for describing your service offering.

This includes job titles. Some organizations get creative with job titles to the extent they no longer describe what that position actually does, or the title doesn't relate to the client organization. If that's the case, abandon your internal job descriptions and use ones that are common to the industry. You can explain how your job descriptions relate to the one you're using within your proposal.

Speaking the client's language may be a problem when subject matter experts or subcontractors write the text. Carefully review what they've written and adapt it to match the client language and consistency with other sections.

Examples they can relate to

Telling stories and using examples to illustrate your point is a powerful way to get the message across and demonstrate your capabilities.

The examples you use should be easily understood by the reviewer and match the message you're trying to convey. The client should also be able to link them to your services and the evaluation criteria, even if you need to point the connection out directly. Don't be afraid to identify how the example supports the evaluation criteria or where it fits into the evaluation framework.

Keep stories and examples short and concise, focusing on the purpose, and eliminating extra information or parts of the example that don't matter to the client. Even if you have to change names or eliminate references to your existing or past clients to maintain anonymity, as long as you position the example properly and it's real, it won't matter.

Instead of including examples within the body of your text in a narrative format, either give the examples a heading, or indent the text to highlight the fact that it's an example. You can also include the examples in a text box that keeps it separate from the main body. Either of these methods will highlight the example without breaking the flow of your proposal text.

Example

Include your example this way:

How we helped another client

Your situation is similar to that of another of our clients. Our new processes cut their turnaround time down from five to two business days. They used this improvement as a selling feature with their own clients, and have attributed a 23 percent increase in orders directly to our service improvements.

Reflect back to them

An effective way to communicate is to reflect back to the client things and phrases they used. This links what you're saying directly with the client's own thoughts, while also reminding the client of the purpose of the information.

This includes repeating the RFP question as the headings in your response, and starting your first sentence with a paraphrase of the information the client is looking for.

Example

Use a simple mirroring technique:

Their question: "Explain how you maintain quality control for your services."

Your answer: "Our process maintains quality control and delivers consistent results to you by... "

Be careful not to take this idea too far. Be subtle and don't simply repeat back the client's own information or entire sentences.

Example | **Don't overdo mirroring:**

A proposal response included almost a full page that repeated the background information from the RFP document.

The intent was to explain that the bidder understood the background, however repeating the information didn't contribute to the evaluation, and probably bored the evaluators.

Refer to them directly

The use of the word 'you' when trying to persuade others is a very powerful sales tool and you should use it. Most proposal writers refer to clients using their company name, if they even refer to them at all. When making a point or trying to demonstrate the value or benefits of your services, simply use the word 'you' to make it personal and speak directly to the client.

Example | **Make it about them, not you:**

In one example a company started most sentences with their own name. For example, "our company can do these things for you."

A better way to say the same thing is by using the words "you will get these benefits from our company... "

By simply flipping around the reference and focusing on the client rather than your company, what you say will have more impact and influence. It makes it easier for the client to personalize your message.

Don't waste their time

As with everybody, time is important to the evaluators. While the evaluation of the RFP proposal responses is important to the client, the evaluators will spend only as much time as they feel is necessary to evaluate it.

If you've made the evaluation a long and tedious exercise for them, the evaluators won't make the extra effort to find the information and points that give you a better evaluation score.

As discussed earlier, don't include information that isn't relevant to the evaluation process unless there's another compelling reason. Resist the temptation to include more in your proposal simply because you can. By sticking to the information that will influence the evaluators and allow them to score you effectively, it will make the evaluation process quicker and easier, and prevent your message from getting buried in non-essential information.

If there's detailed information you feel should be included, put it in the appendix. Don't simply refer the reviewers to the appendix, however, since it makes them stop the flow of their review to find the appendix, locate the specific item, and relate it back to the text they just read. Then the evaluators need to start again where they left off.

Instead, include an introduction and explain the relevance of the document or information in the appendix. Provide a summary or high-level version in the main document, and simply indicate that more details are available in the appendix and provide the location.

Turn facts into messages

Providing facts or nuggets of information is a good way to demonstrate your capabilities, but facts on their own don't contribute to the message you're trying to deliver. Instead, relate the fact directly to the client, the service you're delivering and the scoring criteria. Turn the fact into a benefit and take the time to describe exactly why. If the facts are somewhat obscure or hard to relate to, provide an example or give the fact some context.

Do You Have Any Idea How to Write and Edit?

While the success of your proposal is based primarily on your solution and the strategy you employ, unless the written proposal is well structured, clear, concise and effectively communicates your position, you'll have a harder time getting a positive evaluation.

Writing a proposal is unique. It's not the same as writing a business case, letter or memo. A proposal is a careful balance between a sales pitch and concrete information, and has a very specific purpose. Because of the one-way nature of the process, the written proposal is often your only chance to sell your services, so how you write your proposal is critical to getting a higher evaluation score than your competition.

Forget what you learned in school

Some of the traditional approaches for writing that you learned in high school or in a college business writing course don't fit the needs of a persuasive proposal, and are more appropriate for other forms of writing.

When writing a proposal, you're not trying to sound smart. You're not trying to demonstrate your understanding of the English language, grammar rules or sentence structure. You're writing to communicate clearly, and influence the evaluator.

While elements of grammar are important for communication to avoid confusion and misunderstanding, it's more important to communicate effectively than to follow all the rules without question.

Tip | Writing that is grammatically correct but hard to read is much less effective than simple, plain language.

Everyone has an editor

Even the best writers have editors, and anything you, your subject matter experts or subcontractors write for the proposal should be edited by someone else. When most people write, they usually write about what they know. This doesn't always translate into good writing that's well explained, because we subconsciously know things we don't include, or we structure text in a way we understand, but that isn't clear to others.

Someone else will be able to see these problems as well as identify spelling, grammar and other mistakes you don't see.

Writing to Persuade, Not Sedate

Reviewers have to read a large amount of information from each company submitting a proposal response. You want the reviewers to focus their attention on your proposal so they can remember what they read and relate it to the RFP requirements and scoring criteria so they can score your proposal.

Writing that is short, snappy, to the point, easy-to-read and visually appealing will get the reviewer's attention.

Writing that is long-winded and complex with large blocks of text and no visual cues to show the reviewers where the important information is will strain the reviewer's eyes and lose their attention.

In addition, you need to write so that the material is interesting. That's why examples and stories are important, as are visual material such as flow charts, illustrations and other graphics that provide information and do more than just fill space.

Example

This is long-winded and difficult to read:

We appreciate Horticulture and Snow and Ice Removal services are key to not only the aesthetics of the property but more importantly to the functionality and safe use of the property. Well-kept grounds and approaches reflect positively on the owner and we recognize the necessity for functionality, full accessibility and safety throughout.

This is short and focuses on the message:

Visual appearance, the safety of occupants and accessibility are important to our reputation and to your image. We use planned, efficient services and processes to achieve this.

The goal is to get your message across and persuade the reader to select you. That persuasion will only work if isn't hidden in long, difficult-to-read and boring language or marketing fluff.

There are easy techniques you can use to make your material easier to read:

- ✓ Use simple, descriptive words.
- ✓ Start sentences with action.
- ✓ Keep sentence and paragraphs short.

Another way to persuade rather than sedate is to provide clear, concise summaries of the information, and stay away from wishy-washy terminology. Focus on action, and put images in the minds of the reader that demonstrate what you can do.

Example

This isn't very convincing, partly because of the use 'anticipate' and 'would':

> "We anticipate that the people dedicated to your portfolio would include qualified, seasoned team members, new hires, and existing employees currently involved in similar services."

This is better, because it provides details and certainty:

> "Three current employees with experience providing the same service for other clients will transfer to your account. They will hire two new employees with at least five years experience in your specific industry, and be trained on our system and procedures before they start."

Don't start your proposal, executive summary, cover letter, responses to questions, etc., with a long-winded platitude, a rehashing of the process or RFP information. Start with a quick description of the problem and follow immediately with your solution. The reviewers want to see what you have to say, not get a repeat of what they've told you.

Write From the Client's Point of View

An effective proposal is written from the client's point of view. By doing this, you will develop information and write it so it's relevant to the client and their interests, not yours. You will be able to get your message across much better this way.

First, this approach will force you to understand the client's point of view. This comes from your research and your strategic planning. Second, the client will receive your message much better if you developed it to fit their point of view. Since the message will match the client's concerns, background and interests, they will understand and absorb it more easily. From a client perspective, this demonstrates that you understand the client, and that your approach to business is client-focused.

Writing from the client's point of view is often difficult for subject matter experts and technical people. They have a hard time divorcing their enthusiasm, interests and what they feel is more interesting from what the client is interested in or how the client would look at a given issue. Take some extra time to coach these contributors or closely review their material and adjust it to the client's point of view. This includes reducing technical details and providing information that matters to the client.

How you address this will be based on the strategic planning you did earlier to understand the client.

Too Much Detailed Information

It's easy to pack lots of information into your proposal, especially when writers know and are passionate about the topic. This detailed information may distract from the message.

Some material, however, simply isn't needed and should be eliminated. Don't be afraid to throw out content that doesn't support your message and influence the evaluators.

To minimize the amount of information you include, prioritize the material and then eliminate the low priority material based on its potential influence and impact on the evaluators, including its relevance to the evaluation criteria and the scoring matrix.

Be sure that the information you do use is important to the evaluation, not simply important to you. Don't use material that doesn't support your message. This may mean cutting out material that has been provided by others.

For the information you do use, put it where it matters. Use the techniques described earlier to split the information between the main body and the appendix.

In addition to using format and structure to identify the most important information, start with summaries and condensed information that is followed by supporting details. Finish with a summary, repeating the key message.

Tip | Use the tried and tested approach: tell them what you're going to tell them, tell them, and then tell them what you told them.

Are You Still Using a Typewriter?

There's a simple reality you face when writing a proposal response: there's a limited time you have to complete and deliver it before the deadline. No matter how long you're given, from the time the RFP is issued to the deadline for submitting, it won't be enough.

A big time-waster can be formatting the proposal and integrating various pieces. A well-formatted and well-structured proposal needs consistency throughout the entire document and well thought out headings and sub-headings, not to mention text for captions, text boxes, bullet points, lists, headers and footers, and many other elements.

The easiest way to reduce the time and effort it takes to do this while increasing your flexibility and the visual appearance of your proposals is to use your word processor's features to their fullest capabilities.

When it comes to writing a proposal, two of your word processor's most useful features are generating an automatic table of contents and formatting styles. These features are available in leading word processors such as Pages, MS Word for Apple, and MS Word for PC. Even the free open source word processing software OpenOffice has these features.

Styles save you effort and improve consistency

Styles are standard formatting that you can apply to any text within your document. When you change the style, every occurrence of that style in your document changes automatically. You can create different levels of headings, for instance, and if you want to change the font size, color, typeface or indents, all you do is change the style once and everything with that style changes with it. If you don't like the way it looks, simply change it back.

You can set up your format in advance, and then make changes easily to adjust the visual representation of your document. You can easily apply a style, either by selecting the style or using the formatting brush to copy the style. Some discipline at the start of the process will save you lots of time at the end.

An advantage is that you can create your template with your styles and provide that template to anyone who is writing a part of the proposal. When the writers submit their information, you can easily integrate it into the main document since the formatting and the styles will be the same. This makes it much easier. If you've ever cut and paste from several documents you understand the headaches if you aren't organized in advance.

This works very well if you have a large proposal with individual sections that are being worked on separately. It's easier to merge documents when they all have the same styles.

Save time with an automatic table of content

Your table of contents can be automatically generated, saving you time and potential errors. With this feature, page numbers are always right, and if you change the document, updating the table of contents is just a simple command.

Styles are a key part of the automatic table of contents. By tagging each heading with a particular Table of Contents level, the word processor generates the table of contents along with the correct page number. After you make changes to the document, re-generate the table of contents. This is quicker and less prone to error than manually creating the table of contents at the end.

Should You Use a Professional Writer?

It really depends on the size and extent of the proposal response. Even if you don't hire a writer to develop the proposal text, it's useful to have a writer review the final proposal and edit it for you. Using writers at the final stage of the process will add value with less cost, and provide you with even better base material for the next proposal. Don't forget to review the changes to make sure they don't change the context.

When using a professional writer, even if the writer specializes in proposal responses, remember that the writer doesn't know your company or business. They should supplement your internal efforts, not replace them. You need to write the base content, particularly the operational material. With enough time, a good writer can learn more, interview the subject matter experts, gather the right information and write good material. But the best approach is to create the initial material, and let the writer develop and improve it based on your outline and strategy.

Example

Give writers the information they need:

For a major proposal response, a company used internal staff writers who didn't have any knowledge or history of the service delivery. They also hired external writers with even less knowledge.

The result was well-written but generic material that did not demonstrate knowledge of the client or the company's capability.

Even if you don't use a professional editor, have somebody else within your organization, who is not involved in the RFP process, do a final read and edit for grammar, spelling, punctuation, consistency, and other minor mistakes that are easy to miss. You want the final product to be as clean and error-free as possible. Some evaluators will look at those mistakes and feel that if you can't get these details right in a proposal, how are you going to get the service details right?

If you have several people writing the final version, you can have them edit each other's work. For instance, John writes one particular section, and when he's done with that section it goes to Jane to review and edit. When Jane is finished with her own writing, it goes to John, who edits it.

Use a Writing Process

The best way to write effectively is to use a process. This introduces a structured approach and some discipline, and produces more effective writing with less effort.

The following is a simple process you can use when writing proposals, and can be used for other writing as well.

Reference Info	This process and other reference material is provided separately at the back of the book for you to use as reference.

The POWER system for writing

Prepare

1. Establish the message.
2. Create your SOCO (Single Overriding Communication Objective).
3. Analyze the audience.
4. Decide on messaging, themes, hot buttons, and solution.
5. Collect your facts and supporting information, including images, samples, examples, etc.
6. Create compelling arguments.

Outline

1. Develop the overall structure and flow of your proposal response.

2. Define the headings and sub-headings that will cover all the information you need to include.
3. Identify the important information that needs to be highlighted.
4. Establish where tables, illustrations, bullet lists, etc., need to support your message.

Write/Wait

1. Use the outline to start filling in the information and writing the material.
2. Don't initially self-edit. Get all your information down on paper.
3. Periodically go back and compare your material with the original message and your outline.
4. Wait or move on to another section, leaving at least a full day before coming back to edit what you've written.

Edit

1. Read your original writing from top to bottom.
2. Do a rough edit on content, structure and format. Be brutal. Don't be afraid to delete material that doesn't matter (copy to another document just in case).
3. Do a final edit and then check style and spelling.
4. Have someone else review your text and give you feedback.
5. Edit again.

Review

1. Reread your newly edited material. Be critical.
2. Compare your text with your message, SOCOs, themes, hot buttons, and the evaluation criteria.
3. Edit again if necessary.

Win With Format and Structure

The format and structure of your proposal are an important part of what persuades the evaluators. Unless the evaluators are able to clearly see what you're saying, the efforts you put into your proposal strategy and content will be ineffective.

Why is format and structure so important?

A persuasive proposal should lead the evaluator to the arguments and messages, all in an effort to convince them that you should be selected as the successful bidder.

Structure is the visual representation of the information, and includes headings, placement of graphics, and positioning of key information. It also includes how you organize your proposal, for example what information you provide and in what order.

Format is the size and font of your text, margins, headings and sub-headings. It's the indenting, bullets, and other visual clues you provide to the text and the overall document.

Structure and format provide the following benefits:

- ✓ Visually easier to read and helps retention.
- ✓ Leads the evaluator to your message.
- ✓ Focuses attention on what you want the evaluator to see.

The overall structure of your document and each separate section should be planned. This includes the following elements:

- Lead-in.
- Detail/facts/arguments.
- Summary or conclusion.

This basic information structure can be repeated throughout your proposal document.

Create a structure

Having great content that connects your message to the evaluators, demonstrates your capabilities, and matches the evaluation criteria is wasted if the reviewer doesn't see it. While you can hope the reviewers read everything, reading and seeing information are two different things. You must structure the information so that it's compelling and easy to read.

Start with compelling headings and always start with a powerful first sentence or paragraph. Don't save the best content for the last paragraph, or the evaluators may never read it. The idea is to get the evaluators interested and focused on the information so they can link it to their evaluation process.

Develop a flow for your entire proposal and for each section or question you respond to. Use the same structure so that it becomes familiar to the reviewer and easier to read and absorb. The reviewer will become familiar with where you put information, and will be able to anticipate it as they read the full proposal.

To promote this consistent approach, structure each question with the same sub-headings. The headings you choose depend on the requirements in the proposal and client requirements. They may even be expanded for specific questions. Here are some examples you can use as headings:

- ✓ Introduction to our service delivery
- ✓ Our advantages
- ✓ How we manage the service
- ✓ How we deliver the service
- ✓ Our Quality Control is built-in
- ✓ Experience with current clients
- ✓ Technology and processes we use
- ✓ Alignment with your criteria
- ✓ Benefits you receive
- ✓ Summary of our capabilities

By using introductions and summaries, you also help the evaluator know what they're about to read and then summarize what they've just read. This will make it easier for the evaluator to relate to the material. Also, don't be afraid to repeat important content or messages.

Under each heading in your outline, identify how you plan to respond, what examples, graphics or information you will include, and list the hot buttons, messages, or key phrases.

When you start the writing process, provide the outline to the review team to get their initial comments and suggestions. They may be able to provide some additional guidance and advice before you start filling in the blanks.

Techniques

Visibly separating out information to make it easier to read and absorb while relating it to the overall message is one of the reasons for format and structure. Here are several techniques you should use in your proposal to achieve those goals.

Chunking

This involves pulling out key information from your main text and separating it out. You can use a text box, an indented paragraph, separate graphic, or a table to do it.

By using a text box in Microsoft Word, for instance, the main text can wrap around the main text. Using shading, borders or a bold title will draw attention to it.

Get attention

By using a text box, you can focus attention on a key point.

This is an excellent way to place key information in a highly visible manner. Don't be afraid to repeat material from your main text using this technique.

Bookends

Bookends are a powerful tool that draws attention to your message outside of the main flow of the text.

Bookends go at the beginning and end of each question or section. They are short and powerful and have a focused message. Add bookends before and after your introduction and conclusion whenever possible. For short questions, bookends can replace the introduction and conclusion.

When using bookends, put them in a box, shade them, or use other formatting techniques such as italics or a larger font to separate them from the main text. Usually, bookends are short and sum up the key point or main message. Different wording should be used for each end of the bookend, but they should reflect one another. This reinforces your message through repetition, and also provides a short, simple, obvious message that the evaluator is more likely to read and remember.

The advantage of using bookends is that they:

- ✓ Frame your point.
- ✓ Are the first and last paragraphs or statements, therefore are most likely to read and remembered.
- ✓ Repeat your key message and selling points.

As a powerful tool, bookends help get your message across through repetition and a highly visible format.

Signposts

Signposts are visual references. They point the reviewer to information you want them to see, and provide a reference point for transitions. The most obvious example of this is headings and sub-headings. By breaking up your text with headings and sub-headings, which describe the content that will follow, you're using signposts.

White space	Use white space and visual separation around key points and items you want to bring attention to, such as customer testimonials.
Headings	**Meaningful headings draw attention** ***Sub-headings structure information***
Bullet points	☑ Bullet points can get attention. ✖ Bullet points can say something.
Bold text	When used sparingly, bold text can emphasize something **within** a paragraph.
Images	Charts, diagrams and figures illustrate your point. **Success rates**

Boxing

Boxing involves separating information using a table structure that enables you to focus attention, and organize the information so it's easy to see. Boxing follows a specific structure that makes it easier to follow and understand. Tables are easy to use and can be inline with the text as shown below, or float with wraparound similar to the text box used in the Chunking example.

<table>
<tr><td>Visually separate information</td><td>It separates out the information visually, separating it from the main narrative.</td></tr>
<tr><td>Easy to find</td><td>Instead of being buried in the text, the information is easy to find.</td></tr>
<tr><td>Organized structure</td><td>The technique allows you to easily organize information you might otherwise have included in a hard-to-read paragraph.<table>
<tr><td>Step 1</td><td>Decide how to structure your information.</td></tr>
<tr><td>Step 2</td><td>Create a table with the columns and rows.</td></tr>
<tr><td>Step 3</td><td>Enter your information.</td></tr>
<tr><td>Step 4</td><td>Format the text and the table.</td></tr>
</table></td></tr>
</table>

When using these techniques, use them consistently so the same kind of information, such as an example or benefit, always looks the same and is easily recognizable.

The look and feel of your proposal

Make the entire proposal easier to read with lots of white space and visual cues such as headings, tables, diagrams and bullet lists described above to enhance concepts and relationships between information. Avoid long blocks of text, which are hard to read. Split long blocks of text into shorter paragraphs or use sub-headings.

This approach highlights information and gives the reviewer easy-to-find information. While these techniques are often seen in magazines and newspapers, they are powerful when used in a proposal, and can help you pull out important material from the main body of text.

Where possible, use color to provide visual cues and make your proposal more interesting to look at. Don't overdo it, however, as it can become a distraction.

Essentially, you're guiding the evaluators to your message with these visual cues, and focusing their attention on what you want them to see. The white space and visual cues also require less effort and will create less fatigue on the evaluator.

Your Writing Style Matters

The style you use in your proposal influences how easy the information is seen and remembered by the evaluator. Don't try to impress with your writing – you aren't writing a novel. Long sentences and fancy grammar detract from your message and make it harder for the evaluator to fully absorb your message.

Shorten your sentences and use more paragraphs for longer written material, keeping only one or two concepts or thoughts per paragraph. Simplify your sentences using fewer words, and get rid of excess words.

Tip | In *Words That Work*, Dr. Frank Luntz advocates simple language and small words to get your message across.

Keep it simple and eliminate extra words

When most people write, they usually write like they speak. Often, this involves looser language with more complicated phrases, longer words and filler words. It's worst when the writer feels that fancy language conveys a sense of importance or intelligence. The editing process helps you eliminate such phrases and words, all of which make it harder to understand what you mean.

Some examples include:

Hard to absorb	Easy to absorb
In view of the fact that...	Because
In the event that...	If
Involves the use of...	Uses
Institute	Begin/start
To this end, we want you to	Please...
...so that you...	... so you...
Will be able to...	Can
Will include	Includes
To be able to	To

No buzzwords!

Every industry has buzzwords and special terms, and many companies have their own. Sometimes, the interpretation is not exactly the same to everyone, which can lead to problems. Also, while using these terms may be appropriate to the client, if you aren't careful, they could make it harder to communicate. It's better to use plain English to describe what you mean, and avoid buzzwords when you can.

Picture language

It's much more powerful to describe what you mean than use a single word. It doesn't mean you should describe everything, but the more descriptive you are, the more interesting the reading will be to the evaluator, and the easier it will be for them to form an image in their mind and therefore remember the details they need to evaluate you.

Using picture language includes describing abstract numbers in terms that are easy to visualize. Your descriptions should relate to the client and the industry, and what makes sense to them. Sometimes, the numbers themselves are so commonly used, they can stand on their own.

Example

Make your example easy to visualize:

Our service saves two tons of paper per year, equivalent to 12 delivery vans filled with paper worth over $8,000.

Our technicians receive refresher training each year, totaling six full working days.

Using picture language will improve your message. Its benefits are:

- Non-technical language is easier to understand.
- Illustrating with picture language supports your message.
- It makes it easier to put something in the evaluator's perspective in a way that demonstrates benefits.
- You can include comparisons and examples the evaluator can imagine.

Short paragraphs, short sentences

When reading, we need a break between thoughts to properly absorb information. Paragraphs are the tools used to break up a longer section into separate ideas or pieces of information. These are easier to see and read if there's a visible break in between. You can improve the understanding even more by adding headings.

Sentences should also be relatively short to help comprehension and make the proposal less tiring to read. Don't make the sentences too short and choppy, though, since this will make the flow difficult and the message won't be continuous.

Use active sentences

Use active language to show action. Avoid passive language, which uses more words and is harder to read and understand. Active language also conveys a more powerful, action-oriented impression. The benefits include:

- Easier to read.
- Positive impression on evaluators.
- Shows action and eliminates doubt.

Passive language	Active language
We are looking forward to working with you and implementing the new policy.	We will implement the policy with you.
Our service will enable…	Our service enables…
Information is going to be provided in the meeting.	You will receive information at the meeting.

When required by the circumstances, we can provide prompt services	We provide prompt service.
The air was tested by the specialist.	The specialist tested the air.
Further to receiving your drawings, specifications and details, we would like to take this opportunity to advise that we approve the submitted drawings provided.	We approve the work based on the information submitted.
Upon approval of the business case, it would be our intent to commence working towards improvement of services right away.	With your approval, work to improve services can start immediately.

Go Fishing

For many reviewers, the executive summary will be the first thing they read. This is your opportunity to hook the evaluator with your executive summary, and then sell them with your proposal by putting forward your advantages and the reason they should select you. You should also tell the reviewers what you will demonstrate in your proposal that will make them want to select it as the winning proposal.

While the executive summary should be short, two pages are also appropriate if the content includes headings, short paragraphs and other visual cues, all of which typically require more space. While it's a powerful tool, don't rely on the executive summary. Some reviewers won't read it – they'll go directly to your proposal.

Use the same techniques for the executive summary that you use for the main proposal. It doesn't need to look like a typical dense and dull summary.

Be direct and tell the reviewers why they should choose you. Provide evidence and use the information from your strategic planning, including hot buttons, themes and issues.

Be clear and concise about what differentiates you from the others, and what benefits they will receive if they select you.

Managing the Production Process

Proposal production may be done by a specific individual who has experience in the process, or it may be left up to you. Either way, it's the last step of the process, but requires considerable preplanning to get it right and do it on-time.

Requirements can vary considerably, depending on the size of the proposal, the number of copies, and even the proposal's importance. Sometimes the production and delivery requirements are very specific, and must be followed exactly to avoid being disqualified.

This part of the process includes arranging for printing, deciding on the look and layout of binder covers, producing tabs, and possibly even producing some additional material that's included with the proposal, such as corporate information.

The production might include burning a softcopy of the proposal documentation onto a DVD, or even producing a multimedia presentation to supplement the proposal.

Printing

For production, it's important to understand the total duration of time it will take to print, assemble and do a quality check. If you use an external company to do your production, make sure they can deliver on your deadlines and whether they're willing to work overnight if necessary. This kind of flexibility may be necessary.

Shipping/Delivery

Once it's been produced, the proposal has to be delivered on time. Whenever possible, your proposal should be delivered in person because that provides you with the greatest degree of control, and ensures the proposal gets to the destination on time.

If, because of geography or time, the proposal needs to be sent by courier, it's important to understand the pick-up and delivery timelines. When possible, try to deliver your proposal ahead of time to avoid events that are beyond your control, causing your submission to be disqualified because it's submitted late.

Lessons Learned

Send your proposal early and track it's progress:

A supplier used a well-known courier to deliver a proposal to the client in another city. With an overnight guarantee of delivery by 12 noon, and a 3pm submission deadline, the package went missing. The bidder found out about it too late because they weren't tracking the submission. They were disqualified.

Example

Invest in on-time delivery:

A very large proposal covered nine separate regions and each region had a separate proposal that was 1,000 pages in length.

Seven copies were required for each region, meaning the full proposal had sixty-three 1,000 page documents. Each proposal was split into two-3" binders. The financial proposal was in a separate 1" binder with three copies for each region. This made for a total of 153 binders.

Instead of couriering the proposals to the city where they were to be received, the company rented a van and sent two employees to drive four hours each way. This delivery was done two days in advance just in case there was an accident and another set would need to be sent.

Summary

Your strategy, benefits and great content need to get in front of the client and the evaluators, and the written form of your proposal is the interface. By understanding how hard it is to communicate effectively, and knowing how to influence the evaluator with well-structured writing, and important techniques to make your proposal hit the mark and stick in the minds of the client, you will have the edge over your competition.

Techniques You Can Use:

- ✓ Use structure to make sure your benefits and value are seen.
- ✓ Know what will influence the evaluators and focus on it.
- ✓ Use a writing process to translate your content onto paper.
- ✓ Implement techniques to highlight key messages.

Traps To Avoid:

- ✖ Don't write to impress, write to influence.
- ✖ Don't hide your message behind unimportant information.
- ✖ Don't write what you want, write for the client.

Your Action Plan to Write Better Proposals:

Based on this chapter, list several things you need to do or must do differently to win more business with your proposals.

Priority	Things to Do

Part 8 Things Clients Want You to Know

While clients are all different, there are some basic things they expect from your proposal responses, whether it's stated up front or not.

In most cases, it's about making the proposal easy to read and evaluate - something that's equally important to bidders. Unfortunately, too many bidders write their proposals without considering the client.

Here are examples and advice straight from client organizations and evaluators. Some are already discussed earlier in the book, but it doesn't hurt to know they come directly from the client.

In all cases, the information has been edited to eliminate reference to projects or clients, and rewritten into a consistent format.

> *"All men make mistakes, but only wise men learn from their mistakes."*
>
> *– Winston Churchill*

Differentiate Yourself

This is one of the most important things to get right. RFPs exist so clients can decide between various bidders and make a final selection. If you haven't given the client what they need to differentiate you from others, you haven't written a winning proposal.

> *"Many of the good responses were from firms that quoted what was requested, but also highlighted additional benefits that differentiated them. The responses also provided alternatives, which were sometimes a better alternative for our needs."*

> *"The bidder's worst crime is failing to answer the key question, and instead regurgitating their key selling point."*

> *"Many features are discussed and identified by bidders, but there's usually no corresponding, clearly identified benefit."*

> *"There's no consistent theme of 'why us' – lots of features and claims, but there isn't anything that demonstrates their value."*

> *"What's impressive is good format, solid answers and something a little out of the ordinary, such as insight into the industry that we haven't seen from the other bidders. In other words, provide more than is expected."*

> *"We like bidders to be responsive to the questions, and do a little research on us, and then impress us with their insight."*

Skip the Sales Pitch

This is particularly important if you've been invited to bid or have received the RFP through a pre-qualification process. The client knows you have the size, capacity and sophistication they need, so you don't have to sell your company to them. You simply have to answer their questions and give them the facts and evidence they need to compare you to the other bidders.

"From a buyer's viewpoint the biggest issue is that suppliers can't resist the sales pitch in the RFP, even though they've been told not to. Why waste time, words and paper trying to convince us that they're good enough to be considered? If we had any doubts you wouldn't have gotten this far. Just stick to the point. Cutting down the size of proposals will make your proposal easier to read."

"A solid answer is what we need, with information we can evaluate on. When we ask a question, it's usually for a purpose. If the question has been looked at thoughtfully to understand the reason for the question before answering, you're more likely to get it right."

Follow the Format

If the RFP requires you to follow a particular format, or encourages you to use the same order as the questions, do what you're told. The client expects it and probably has a reason – it might be to match up answers with evaluation criteria. If you don't follow directions in the RFP, the client will wonder what you're like to work with.

"When a bidder doesn't follow the format or the order of the questions in the RFP request, they probably just used boilerplate material and didn't care enough about the business to customize it."

"When they don't follow the format, it makes the evaluation very tough – they shouldn't make evaluators do the work for them."

"Answer everything that's asked for in the order it was asked – there may be a reason."

"I really like to read bids that follow the format given and answer exactly what was asked for."

"You should reiterate the question briefly and then answer it – tell the reader what the section will contain and then follow it. If you need to provide additional information, tell us what and why."

"Respond in the format we provide, since that's usually how we have our analysis set up. Any other response makes more work for us, and taints the perception of you as a supplier."

"We appreciate it when the service provider respects the format we've asked them to follow. Every so often they do something different, but it doesn't usually work."

Understand the Requirements

When writing the RFP response, make sure you know what you're writing about, and even more importantly, what you're pricing. Clients will notice if you don't, and wonder if they'll get what they expect.

"The biggest challenges are with bidders who do not read the material provided. Questions and specifications are complete and accurate, yet bidders still don't listen to what they've been asked for."

"Inevitably at least one of the bidders didn't read everything that was provided to them in the RFP. The question for the bidder is whether they're lazy, stupid or illiterate? Ultimately a bidder like this just takes up time."

"In many of the bids there was very little reference or tie-in with the specification requirements or the nature of the work in the bidder's discussion."

"Don't unilaterally decide to upgrade or downgrade the specifications. Unless we've asked for alternative proposals, you need to match the specification exactly in your proposal. If you want to do something different, add it as an alternative, but make sure you respond to the original requirements first."

Don't Assume Familiarity

While it shouldn't be a sales pitch, you need to tell the client your strengths and benefits. Don't assume they'll know this simply because of your company name. This applies even if you're the incumbent.

> *"Just because we know you, doesn't mean you shouldn't remind us in your proposal. Sometimes, the proposals are evaluated by individuals who may not know your company, or are evaluating strictly based on what's written, not background knowledge. You risk a lower evaluation by making that assumption."*

Don't Give Us Marketing Fluff

Always assume your buyer is sophisticated and won't be swayed by a marketing pitch. Using marketing fluff and empty statements won't be well received, and leaves you less room for the more important things you need to tell the client.

> *"Proposals that constantly refer to public information or marketing material and make no real attempt to show how they will meet the requirements won't get a favorable review."*

> *"You can assume that the company doesn't have an answer when there's lots of fluff in their response. It puts their capabilities into question."*

> *"Some important material was well hidden and couldn't be found easily in a proposal. It simply took too much time and effort to find and evaluate it."*

> *"Fluff just gets glossed over. If important, meaty information is hidden in the fluff and is missed, too bad."*

> *"Make your answers to-the-point, in very plain language and backed-up with details. Don't fill them with useless information and fluff."*

"Don't put fluff or fillers in the answers – tell us your approach and back it up."

"Don't use too many statements such as world-class, state of the art, best in class, etc., without evidence. These are empty phrases."

Show Us That You Care

It does take effort to write a proposal, but you must put in the effort to show your client you'll deliver if you're selected. By not considering the client, the evaluators and the process, you're weakening your chances of success, since they will wonder what kind of effort you'll put into the work once you get it.

"Don't load us down."

"Don't put us to sleep."

"Show that our business is important to you."

"Getting too weighty a volume is irritating – we prefer concise answers."

"Getting the response in on time is critical. If someone just misses the deadline by a couple of minutes, it puts people in an awkward position, especially if there are a limited number of suppliers and we want enough bidders to be competitive."

"Don't have your senior executives put a call into our senior executives when you're told in the RFP to deal with a specific contact. If they go to the top during an RFP process, it makes the evaluators question how hard it will be to deal with you once you have the contract."

"Sometimes bids are submitted by one part of the organization and then another will call to see if there are any opportunities. This suggests that the company is not very well coordinated."

"Very poor bids have been submitted by good companies. Sometimes one team or group runs with it to keep the opportunity for themselves, without help or resources from the rest of the organization. There's no visibility with senior management, and the bid doesn't get the attention it deserves."

"When asked for a point of contact, make sure the point of contact is always available. If asked for one contact, don't provide several."

*"Keep it as short as possible. If you're given a **10**-page limit for an answer and don't need **10** pages, use only eight."*

"Sometimes they leave a question blank with no answer given. It makes it impossible to give any score. Depending on the question, it may look like they're being evasive. Never leave anything unanswered, or ambiguous."

Don't Use Boilerplate Material

It's obvious to evaluators when you use boilerplate material, and suggests you don't care about the business very much, or haven't really thought about what you'll do for the client. Always submit a customized proposal.

*"Perhaps the most annoying habit is sending back a **15**-page proposal where **13** pages of it is boilerplate. Bidders should spend the time on the front end submitting a proposal that is unique and has unique solutions."*

"A bidder left in references to another project in their bid. Take the time and show you care about our project."

"If you use boilerplate material, edit it properly."

"Use the appendix for additional information and boilerplate material, or add it to the end of a section so it doesn't distract us from understanding what you can do, but still provides support and gives evidence."

What Not to Do

Here is a sampling of observations from real proposals that illustrate mistakes others have made.

- The proposal still has the term 'NTD' in the final submission. (The NTD means 'Note to Draft' and should be eliminated before finalizing the document.)
- The beginning of many responses takes up the first full line of text with the name of the bidding team, including acronyms.
- The following fluff was written in a proposal: "actively engage with Client's vision to create a central organizational hub that allows Client to draw on its interdisciplinary strengths in order to pursue a client-centered philosophy within an improved and healthy physical setting."
- This phrase from a proposal is not action-oriented and is in the third person: "technology is the cornerstone of our service delivery". It should be written along the lines of: "We use technology to get results."
- A bidder didn't refer to the specification requirements anywhere in the answer. They could have described how they will do what they're asked. Instead, they talked in general terms that were very generic and boilerplate.
- The word 'philosophy' was used too much in a proposal. For instance, instead of "Good Customer Service," they used "Good Customer Service Philosophy." A philosophy doesn't automatically translate into results.
- A bidder used too much qualifying language, such as "... efforts to ensure that the requirements of the specifications are met." It tells the evaluator that they will try their best, but they aren't very confident in succeeding.
- In one proposal a bidder didn't seem to consider what might be important to the client – they simply pounded their chests about what they could do and how good they were.
- A large proposal described part of the service delivery in a way that didn't match with actual site conditions. It seemed as if they didn't read the scope and simply used boilerplate material.

- One company used the name of their computer system in their description of process without first explaining it. They presumed the evaluators were familiar with the specific application. They weren't, and had a hard time following the document.
- The full question, which had two parts, was not answered. The bidder did the right thing and repeated the question as a header, but it was only the first part of the question. They missed the second part of the question, possibly because the writer didn't have the full question in front of them.
- There were too many cross-references to other sections in one bid. Since sections were evaluated independently by different subject matter experts, and the document was actually split up, the cross-references made it much more difficult for the evaluators, even if they had bothered to follow the references.
- This phrase was used in a proposal: "innovative education and awareness programs proven successful for other clients could be leveraged for your requirements," but it doesn't say anything. The evaluator would have to take it at face value, except that they don't have facts and evidence to support the statement.
- Sometimes bidders say that their approach or solution is 'unique' in the industry, as one recent proposal response did, yet the evaluators knew for a fact that it wasn't unique and had become common practice. This hurt the bidder's credibility.
- Claiming 'unique expertise' when you're clearly not the only one with that experience or expertise can look like an inflated claim and hurts your overall credibility.

Summary

A successful proposal gives the client and the evaluators what they need to evaluate the proposal. Everything the client tells you or asks for in their RFQ or RFP document is there for a reason. Carefully consider their reasons for everything they ask for and demonstrate your interest in their business and your professionalism through your proposal submission.

Techniques You Can Use:

- ✓ Do what they tell you by following their structure and format.
- ✓ Carefully read the specifications and use them in your response.
- ✓ Customize your proposal – avoid boilerplate and marketing fluff.

Traps To Avoid:

- ✖ Don't underestimate the client.
- ✖ Don't give them a sales pitch.
- ✖ Don't make it hard from them to evaluate you.

Your Action Plan to Write Better Proposals:

Based on this chapter, list several things you need to do or must do differently to win more business with your proposals.

Priority	Things to Do

Quick Reference Material

In this section, we've repeated some key reference material and checklists for your convenience, including the page number where it's originally discussed so you can refer back to the full text for an explanation.

This section puts the checklists and key reference material all in one place and if you want, you can photocopy them or even cut them out to use them for your next proposal.

These checklists are also available on our website. Please refer to the information on the last page for the website address.

The Eight Golden Rules for a Successful Proposal (refer to page 28)

Here are eight simple rules you should use when writing proposals – they will help you focus your efforts and give the client what they expect:

1. Follow instructions when responding to the RFP.
2. Understand what the client wants to hear.
3. Answer the questions the client asks.
4. Have a great solution that solves the client's problem.
5. Be creative about your proposal and solution.
6. Keep the sales pitch to a dull roar.
7. Get your message across clearly and concisely.
8. Make it easy for evaluators to evaluate you positively.

7 Deadly Sins of Writing (refer to page 182)

Here are the 7 deadly sins of writing you need to avoid when writing your proposal:

- ✖ Writing without a plan.
- ✖ Writing what you want to say, not what the audience wants to read.
- ✖ Trying to sound too smart.
- ✖ Writing too much fluff.
- ✖ Following a structure that's hard to read.
- ✖ Making your key message hard to find.
- ✖ Leaving the good stuff for the end.

The Proposal Process (refer to page 32)

A successful proposal follows a process. The key steps in a successful proposal response process include these elements, which will be expanded further below:

1. Pre-RFP issue
2. RFP review
3. Strategy
4. Kick-off
5. Pricing Model
6. Service solution
7. Management solution
8. Style sheet
9. Project plan (resources and schedule)
10. Version control
11. Iteration and consolidation
12. Production and delivery

RFP Review (refer to page 32)

Once you receive the RFP documentation, carefully review the entire RFP to prepare for developing the response and to identify issues, concerns or details that will impact your proposal.

Some of the things you should look for include:

- ☑ The RFP process.
- ☑ Overall timelines.
- ☑ Mandatory requirements.
- ☑ Scoring, evaluation criteria and weighting.
- ☑ Process for submitting questions, including deadlines.
- ☑ Sources of additional information, such as a data room or online source.
- ☑ Site tour dates and other client meetings.
- ☑ The actual scope of work.
- ☑ Specifications and service levels.
- ☑ Financial proposal submission requirements, forms, etc.
- ☑ Technical (written) proposal requirements.
- ☑ Submission (delivery) requirements.
- ☑ Insurance and bonding requirements.
- ☑ Minimum experience requirements.
- ☑ Page count, margins and type size requirements.

Kick-off Meeting (refer to page 36)

Getting everyone on the same page makes it easier to develop an effective proposal. A kick-off meeting gets a proposal project started by giving everyone the information they need, and confirming resources and priorities.

The meeting agenda should include the following elements:

☑ Review the technical proposal requirements (format, etc.) and establish action items if required.

☑ Review the proposal response content requirements, and determine the required proposal format, instructions to writers, etc.

☑ Discuss and assess the response areas to validate and communicate the related hot buttons, key messages and opportunities.

☑ Identify and assess potential internal and external resources who should be followed up to gain adequate information and nuances regarding client needs, expectations and agenda.

☑ Assign key research activities required, both to gain outside information, and for internal information required to respond to the proposal itself.

☑ Provide an initial 'straw-man' organization and solution for the proposal, including both staff and methodology for the service delivery model around which the proposal writers will frame their written material.

☑ Provide writing guidelines, styles, logistics, etc.

☑ Establish writing assignments.

☑ Generate an initial list of questions for the client.

Style Sheet (refer to page 40)

Your style sheet provides information to your proposal contributors, and ensures consistent information. By using a style sheet, you reduce errors, provide a more cohesive proposal to the client, and save a lot of time at the end of the process when you are under pressure to finalize the proposal.

The style sheet should include the following key elements:

- ☑ Basic background information on the client and the overall scope.
- ☑ Document and file naming and numbering conventions.
- ☑ Writing techniques to be used, such as when to expand acronyms, use of headings, formatting of information, etc.
- ☑ How to refer to the client and your company in the written response.
- ☑ Descriptions of the solutions that are important when writing, including processes, names of systems and products, responsibilities, org charts, titles, etc.
- ☑ Client's terminology, acronyms, position titles and other information that needs to be referred to accurately and consistently throughout the proposal.
- ☑ Terminology or issues that should not be discussed or used due to sensitivities or interpretations by the client.
- ☑ Key elements to include in each section or to be answered in questions, such as benefits, examples, process diagrams, etc., to maintain consistency.
- ☑ Hot buttons and issues that should be covered in each section where possible.
- ☑ Format and naming/reference conventions, as well as the format of attachments, images, diagrams and screen shots used in the proposal.

Project Plan (refer to page 41)

No matter how small or large your proposal response will be, you need a project plan with your resources, schedule and tasks identified.

Your proposal response plan should include:

- ☑ All resources needed to complete the proposal response.
- ☑ Timelines and due-dates for all parts of the process, including internal approvals.
- ☑ A process for updating and monitoring progress.
- ☑ Meetings and internal review dates during the process.
- ☑ Logistics (records management and documentation control).
- ☑ Identification of an individual who will provide control and management of the various parts of the proposal.
- ☑ Identification of individuals and their specific tasks or assignments.

Pulling Teeth (refer to page 49)

Even with cooperative resources, getting individuals to contribute in a meaningful way can be challenging. A good way to do this is with a simple form you provide to the contributors.

Include this information for them:

- ☑ Original question from RFP.
- ☑ Short list of hot buttons and solutions you think you need to provide to the client in order to win.
- ☑ The following questions (indicating to the expert that a point form response is acceptable):
    - Why is this solution, method or product valuable?
    - What are the key features that meet client requirements?
    - Where has this been done before successfully?
    - What would be the key steps to implementation?
    - What would be the ongoing interaction and communication with the client after implementation?
    - What information or results, including reporting, can be provided to the client? Provide samples.
    - What analysis and decision-making can come from this information that might be valuable to the client?
    - The client may be concerned with XXX – how would you address this?
    - Are there any existing documents, which could help respond to this question? (Policies and procedures, process diagrams, training material, etc.)

Messages (refer to page 64)

Your proposal response strategy should include key messages that gain support from reviewers, points in the evaluation, and win the proposal.

These messages may include:

- ☑ The level of skills and experience of your staff.
- ☑ How you bring improvement to clients.
- ☑ The benefits of your product or service.
- ☑ How a transition to your company will be seamless.
- ☑ Your advantages over the competition.
- ☑ Your knowledge and understanding of the client's requirements.
- ☑ Your success in achieving the performance requirements or service levels the client is expecting.

Key attributes of your message should be:

- ✓ Impact
- ✓ Relevance
- ✓ Support for your proposal

Questions to Ask Yourself (refer to page 71)

Part of a successful strategy, in addition to the items already discussed, is asking yourself questions about the client and the proposal.

Asking questions is always an easy way to gather information, since the questions force you to examine issues and information.

Some of the questions you should ask include the following:

- ☑ Why are they issuing an RFP now?
- ☑ Who will be reviewing?
- ☑ What is the selection process?
- ☑ What do they need?
- ☑ Who is doing the work now?
- ☑ Do they want change?
- ☑ How are they organized?
- ☑ Who will manage the contract?
- ☑ Who are their clients/customers?
- ☑ What is their core business?

Care and Feeding of Evaluators (refer to page 120)

In most cases, winning a proposal means convincing the evaluators that you deserve the highest score. To ensure you meet the evaluator's requirements, ask yourself these questions:

- ☑ Have you made it easy to evaluate?
- ☑ Have you made your solution clear and easy to understand?
- ☑ Have you demonstrated your capability?
- ☑ Have you structured your proposal logically or in accordance with the requirements?
- ☑ Have you addressed all the evaluation elements?
- ☑ Have you answered all the questions?
- ☑ Have you oversold with fluff?
- ☑ Have you been too arrogant?
- ☑ Have you provided concrete information, or theories and generalities?
- ☑ Have you made it simple?
- ☑ Have you pointed the evaluators to the places you want them to read?

Compliance Matrix (refer to page 174)

Using a compliance matrix as part of your process will ensure you not only address all the questions and information requirements, but also don't miss a technical requirement that could lead to disqualification.

For each question you answer, you could use a checklist that looks like this:

Item to be covered	Introduction	Demonstrate we meet the requirements	Specific past experience	Quality management of services	Reporting and benefits	Resources – who will be involved	Interaction with the client	Benefits of our company's services	Summary	Full review complete?
Question 1										
Question 2										
Question 3										

The POWER System for Writing (refer to page 200)

Prepare

1. Establish the message.
2. Create your SOCO (Single Overriding Communication Objective).
3. Analyze the audience.
4. Decide on messaging, themes, hot buttons, and solution.
5. Collect your facts and supporting information, including images, samples, examples, etc.
6. Create compelling arguments.

Outline

1. Develop the overall structure and flow of your proposal response.
2. Define the headings and sub-headings that will cover all the information you need to include.
3. Identify the important information that needs to be highlighted.
4. Establish where tables, illustrations, bullet lists, etc., need to support your message.

Write/Wait

1. Use the outline to start filling in the information and writing the material.
2. Don't initially self-edit. Get all your information down on paper.
3. Periodically go back and compare your material with the original message and your outline.
4. Wait or move on to another section, leaving at least a full day before coming back to edit what you've written.

Edit

1. Read your original writing from top to bottom.
2. Do a rough edit on content, structure and format. Be brutal. Don't be afraid to delete material that doesn't matter (copy to another document just in case).
3. Do a final edit and then check style and spelling.
4. Have someone else review your text and give you feedback.
5. Edit again.

Review

1. Reread your newly edited material. Be critical.
2. Compare your text with your message, SOCOs, themes, hot buttons, and the evaluation criteria.
3. Edit again if necessary.

References

Made To Stick
Random House, 2007 by Chip Heath and Dan Heath

Yes!: 50 Scientifically Proven Ways to Be Persuasive
Free Press, 2008 by Noah J. Goldstein, Steve J. Martin, Robert B. Cialdini

Words That Work
Hyperion, 2007 by Dr. Frank Luntz

The 22 Immutable Laws of Marketing
HarperCollins, 1994 by Al Ries and Jack Trout

Index

active language, *211*
adapting. *see* proposal styles
appendix, *167*
  extra content, *167*
  large documents, *169*
  referring to, *169*
  too much, *167*
attention, *11*
bad rfp
  confusing or ambiguous, *92*
  multiple part questions, *90*
  not asking for experience, *92*
  not enough information, *93*
  questions too broad, *89*
  repetitive questions, *91*
  responding, *89*
balanced, *8*
benefits, *13*, *112*
  making them memorable, *137*
  match client requirements, *113*
  picture language, *210*
  relative to the competition, *135*
  repeat, *131*
  solution, *80*
bidders meetings, *46*
boilerplate, *4*
  one size fits all, *158*
buzz words, *209*
checklist
  compliance, *177*
  for contributors, *50*
  meeting evaluation criteria, *121*
  messages, *64*
  questions you should ask yourself, *71*
  response plan, *43*
  rfp review, *34*
  style sheet, *40*
clarity, *14*
client
  about them, *134*
  failure to respond to needs, *20*
  helping them, *88*
  mirroring, *140*
  problems, *17*
  refer to them, *190*
  solving problems, *142*
  their point of view, *195*
  their process, *75*
  understanding intent, *108*
  what do they want, *61*
  why choose you?, *144*
  why work with you?, *124*
compelling
  examples, *38*
  information, *12*
competitive advantage, *16*
competitor
  ghosting, *135*
  new entry to market, *102*
compliance

matrix, *174*
table, *176*
concerns
negate, *65*
confidence, *117*
consistency, *116*
contact, *33*
content, *157*
boilerplate, *158*
clutter, *170*
contributors, *44*
customized, *6*
from subcontractors, *173*
from subject matter experts, *173*
library, *159*
partner, *48*
contract, *78*
sample, *35*
convincing, *8*
copy editor, *56*
punctuation, *56*
spelling, *56*
credibility, *9*
avoid these claims, *10*
criteria
evaluation, *67*, *76*
evaluation scoring, *83*
customized, *80*
proposal, *6*
solution, *80*
delivery, *45*
dependability, *116*
editor, *193*
espionage, *118*
evaluation
compliance matrix, *174*
pricing, *84*
technical elements, *84*
evaluation criteria, *67*, *76*
weighting, *67*
evaluators
attention span, *181*
care and feeding, *120*
don't waste their time, *191*
influencing, *186*
make their reading easy, *14*
mirroring, *189*
speak their language, *187*
target them, *141*
understanding them, *68*
evidence
support what you say, *160*
examples, *188*
executive summary, *212*
experience, *162*
insufficient, *19*
features, *112*
feedback, *23*
filename structure, *43*
flow charts. see - graphics
fluff, *9*
format, *202*
adhere to it, *74*
benefits, *202*
boxing, *207*
easier to read, *208*
signposts, *206*
techniques, *204*
gantt charts, *168*
ghosting. see - competitor
government procurement, *27*
grammar
forget what you learned, *192*
graphics
1000 words, *166*
graphs. see - graphics
headings
examples, *203*
hot buttons, *62*, *111*
\i writer
using a professional, *199*

illustrations. see - graphics
incumbent
  you, *98*
  your competitor, *101*
influencing evaluators, *186*
information
  face value, *108*
  overload, *181*
  too detailed, *196*
issues, 111
key attributes, *65*
long proposal. see - proposal:size
losing proposals
  debrief, *22*
  feedback, *23*
  why, *22*
mandatory requirements, *73*
marketing, *5*
messages, *64*, *184*
  honest, *139*
  keep them real, *139*
  relevant, *139*
  simple, *138*
messages that stick, *137*
mirror, *18*
mirroring, *140*
  evaluators, *189*
multiple files, *44*
needs
  addressing, *8*
  assessing, *79*
negative issues, *65*
negotiation, *77*
  bidders in parallel, *77*
outline, *183*
page limit
  using graphics, *166*
passive language, *211*
perception, *65*, *122*
  of the client, *122*
  of you, *123*
  outsiders, *10*
persuade, *193*
phrases
  to avoid, *209*
picture language, *210*
planning
  agenda, *36*
  dissecting the rfp, *73*
  pre proposal, *32*
  production, *45*
  project plan, *41*
  proposal kick-off, *36*
  rfp review, *33*
  strategy session, *35*
  style sheet, *40*
  version control, *43*
pricing, *78*
  basic requirements, *39*
  being creative, *110*
  cafeteria, *95*
  model, *81*
  options, *79*, *82*
printing, *213*
process
  proposal development, *32*
  writing, *200*
production, *213*
project management, *46*
proposal
  look and feel, *208*
  one size fits all, *158*
  planning process, *32*
  production, *213*
  simple quotes, *148*
  size, *160*, *184*
  sole source, *149*
  strategy, *35*
  structure, *203*
proposal review
  red team, *51*
proposal styles

adapting, *145*
rfp, *145*
proposal team, *54*
copy editor, *56*
pricing manager, *55*
proposal administrator, *54*
proposal manager, *54*
writer, *56*
questions
answering, *164*
ask yourself, *71*
asking, *72*
tell them anyway, *171*
to ask contributors, *50*
you don't want to answer, *93*
red team. see - proposal review
relationship, *40*
reoi. see - request for expressions of interest
reputation, *10*
request for expressions of interest, *24*
request for information, *24*
request for proposal, *25*
request for qualification, *25*
request for quotation, *27*
request for tender. see - tender
research, *70*
espionage, *118*
evaluator, *70*
response
inconsistent, *21*
response plan, *43*
response strategy, *60*
resumes, *168*
review, *51*
internal, *51*
operation staff, *53*
rfi. see - request for information
rfp
reading between the lines, *109*
rfq. see - request for quotation, see - request for qualification
rft. see - tender
rules
government, *27*
legislation, *77*
procurement, *73*
rules for a successful proposal, *28*
rumors, *65*
sales pitch, *9*
selling, *130*
differentiate yourself, *131*
differentiating, *143*
don't over-sell, *131*
messages that stick, *137*
the steak, *133*
toot your own horn, *130*
service levels, *39*
shipping/delivery, *214*
site tour, *46*
skills
creative, *6*
marketing, *5*
sales, *5*
writing, *7*
sme. see - subject matter experts
sole source, *26*, *149*
pricing options, *96*
proposed content, *152*
solution
develop, *80*
management, *39*
service, *38*
specification sheets, *170*
spelling, *193*
spelling, *199*
stories
experience, *12*
telling, *12*, *172*
strategy, *4*

pricing, *37*
response, *60*
session, *35*
structure, *202*
style sheet, *40*
subject matter expert, *5*, *173*
submission
format, *74*
mandatory requirements, *73*
requirements, *46*
superficial, *18*
surviving bad situations, *98*
swot analysis, *85*
opportunities, *87*
strength, *85*
threats, *87*
weakness, *86*
table of content, *198*
table structure, *207*
template, *45*
tender, *27*
terms, *209*
themes, *61*
typewriter, *197*
unique selling points, *112*
unsolicited proposal. see sole source, *149*
usp. *see* unique selling points
value add, *113*
competitive advantage, *16*
word processor
styles, *197*
table of content, *198*
writer, *56*
writing
7 deadly sins, *182*
clutter, *170*
elements of success, *180*
eliminate extra words, *209*
it's more than just writing, *60*
message, *184*
outline, *183*
process, *200*
strategic, *181*
style matters, *208*
to communicate, *186*
to impress, *21*

About the Author

Michel has written large, successful RFP responses for service providers and has worked with client organizations to develop RFP specifications, questions, evaluation matrices and performance metrics. He has provided advice and training to evaluators and has evaluated RFP responses for small and large initiatives.

Other books by the Author

Managing Facilities and Real Estate – 47 Strategies, Approaches and Leading Practices
Available Summer 2010

Proposal Writing Blog and Podcast Website

www.howtowinmorebusiness.com

Online Content

www.howtowinmorebusiness.com/pwcontent

Author Website, Twitter & Contact

www.successfuel.ca

www.twitter.com/successfuel

Michel@successfuel.ca

Publisher Website

WoodStone Press

www.woodstonepress.com

www.ingramcontent.com/pod-product-compliance
Lightning Source LLC
LaVergne TN
LVHW050618100826
845148LV00011B/1646

* 9 7 8 0 9 8 1 3 3 7 4 0 1 *